SCOUNDRELS AND SALOONS

Whisky Wars of the Pacific Northwest, 1840–1917

RICH MOLE

VICTORIA · VANCOUVER · CALGARY

Heritage House Publishing Company Ltd.
heritagehouse.ca

Library and Archives Canada Cataloguing in Publication
Mole, Rich, 1946–
    Scoundrels and saloons: whisky wars of the Pacific Northwest 1840–1917 / Rich Mole.

(Amazing stories)
Includes bibliographical references and index.
Issued also in electronic format.
ISBN 978-1-927051-78-8

    1. Temperance—Northwest, Pacific—History. 2. Prohibition—Northwest, Pacific—History.
3. Frontier and pioneer life—Northwest, Pacific. 4. Northwest, Pacific—Social conditions. 5. Northwest,
Pacific—Biography. I. Title. II. Series: Amazing stories (Victoria, B.C.)

HV5309.B7M64 2012   363.4'109795   C2012-904117-3

Series editor: Lesley Reynolds
Proofreader: Liesbeth Leatherbarrow

Cover photo: A Renton, Washington, saloon in 1910. The jocular "Wild West" silliness is already a piece
of the mythologized history, but there's nothing phony about the customers, the bartender or, presumably,
the contents of the bottles behind the bar. Image 264, courtesy of the Renton Historical Society.

The interior of this book was produced on 100% post-consumer recycled
paper, processed chlorine free and printed with vegetable-based inks.

Heritage House acknowledges the financial support for its publishing program from the Government
of Canada through the Canada Book Fund (CBF), Canada Council for the Arts and the province of
British Columbia through the British Columbia Arts Council and the Book Publishing Tax Credit.

16 15 14 13 12 1 2 3 4 5

Printed in Canada

Contents

Virtually forgotten in BC today, fast-shooting John Sullivan is a Canadian Wild West hero, yet he was ridiculed in the press and tried for murder. In the US, Sullivan's gun-barrel justice would have been lauded and made legendary.

Prologue

ANTOINE LUCANAGE WAS ON THE RUN—*again. It wasn't Her Majesty's Royal Navy this time, but that maddeningly relentless government man John D.B. Ogilvie. Ogilvie was no prissy public servant. Less than a year before, during BC's biggest manhunt to date, the former Hudson's Bay Company (HBC) trader had been third in command of the outsized posse of "Indian hunters." Ogilvie helped chase renegade Tsilhqot'in who had killed a road crew at Bute Inlet and ambushed a second party 100 miles southeast of Bella Coola. Now, Ogilvie was on a hunt again, and this time his quarry was French-Canadian Antoine Lucanage.*

Everyone on Bentinck Arm—Native and white—knew lean, pox-pitted Lucanage. Fifty years in the future, he would have been called a "bootlegger." In 1865, he was simply called a "whisky trader." Everyone knew bluff, bearded Ogilvie, too, and knew why he was back in Bella Coola. Lucanage's "trade," exchanging what passed for whisky for just about anything the Natives had of value—including, sometimes, their women— was against the laws of the Colony of British Columbia.

A few weeks before, Lucanage had been arrested by Ogilvie and hustled aboard a ship for the trip down to New Westminster's jail. When the vessel tied up on the Fraser River, Lucanage was gone; he had jumped overboard into the swift, swirling waters of Johnstone Strait.

Instead of drowning, Lucanage staggered onto a gravel beach. Instead of dying there of exposure or starvation, he managed to hail Langley, a passing northbound trade schooner. Thankfully, the skipper, a man named Smith, didn't ask too many questions. After a brief stay in Bella Coola, Smith set sail again, unaware that he carried a stowaway. Lucanage planned to emerge from his hiding place (a storage closet in the captain's own cabin) and convince Smith—at gunpoint, if necessary—to land him on the neighbouring Colony of Vancouver Island.

Now, just four hours down Burke Channel, the cabin door opened. Lucanage heard the voices of two men. One voice belonged to Smith, and the captain was talking about him! Lucanage opened the door a crack. A quick glimpse revealed he hadn't escaped Ogilvie after all. Natives—perhaps some of his own former customers—must have paddled the customs agent up to Langley. *There was no easy way out this time. Lucanage pulled a heavy Colt revolver from his belt.*

Stepping clear of the closet, he pointed his weapon at the wide-eyed Ogilvie and fired. The blast rocked the cabin. Through the smoke, Lucanage watched Ogilvie struggle to his feet and then collapse in his chair. Lucanage yanked the cabin door open and made for the deck. Seconds later, crouching behind a forward deck hatch, the whisky trader watched in disbelief as the bloodied government man staggered into view. Behind him stood Smith and Ogilvie's friend, trader Morris Moss, who was drawing his own gun. Lucanage leaped out, knife in one hand, revolver in the other.

Incredibly, the wounded man lunged for him. With Ogilvie's hands locked on his wrists, Lucanage couldn't bring his weapons to bear. He twisted away and headed for the ship's bow. Behind him a gunshot split the air, then another. Morris Moss dashed up, but at that instant, the mainsail boom swung about and catapulted him into the water.

Once Ogilvie's paddlers hauled Moss into their canoe and he regained Langley's deck, he and Smith carried the comatose Ogilvie into the skipper's cabin. Moments later, crewmen realized a skiff was gone—and so was the murderous whisky trader. In the cabin below, Smith and Moss watched helplessly as Ogilvie breathed his last. The government of British Columbia had suffered its first official whisky-war casualty. John Ogilvie would not be the last.

Introduction

IN THE TUMULTUOUS HISTORY OF the Pacific coast of Canada and the United States of America, one constant thread weaves its way through more than 170 years of astounding social and political change. From the days of the fur trade and log cabins through to the development of large cities and 21st-century Internet and smart-phone societies, the issues surrounding the availability of liquor—and the monetary profit from it—link past and present like nothing else.

Since 1840, people on both sides of the international border have suffered through regional and world wars, survived natural disasters and the 1918 Spanish influenza pandemic, endured economic depressions and celebrated

Introduction

new social freedoms and economic affluence. Yet through it all, the contentious issues arising from the manufacture, distribution and sale of liquor remain a constant. The West Coast was home to many "prohibitions," the first enacted years before the California and BC gold rushes.

Liquor defeated many provincial and state politicians but elected others; it pitted small-town folk against big-city residents, gentiles against Jews, Catholic against Protestant and evangelicals against everyone else. It clogged the courts, filled the jails, plunged thousands of families into poverty and destroyed the self-esteem, careers and lives of countless individuals.

Scoundrels and Saloons explores the issues that could not and would not be resolved, revealing why millions of people called reformers, or progressives, fought to abolish and criminalize what we now consider a personal freedom. It does so through the stories of fascinating combatants on both sides of the border.

1

Furs and Firewater

INSIDE A LONG CEDAR-PLANK house situated on a Vancouver Island beach, a Native chief huddled before a smouldering fire and raised his voice in a mournful lament:

> I didn't know that whisky was no good, and still I was
>   drinking it.
> I found out that whisky was no good.
> Come, come closer to me, my slaves,
> And I'll give you a drink of whisky.
> Come closer to me, come closer to me, my slaves.
> We are drinking now, we feel pretty good.
> Now you feel just like me.

* * *

Fort Vancouver chief factor Dr. John McLoughlin faced a vexing conundrum. American traders were the cause of it all. The HBC's licence of exclusive trade, granted by the king of England, meant nothing to them. It was bad enough that Boston peddlers had been sailing up the coast for over 20 years, but now Yankees had climbed over the mountains, taking Native pelts McLoughlin's own clerks should have been bundling up.

It wasn't simply the Americans' intrusion into company territory that troubled McLoughlin. It wasn't their trading acumen either (many mountain men were illiterate bumpkins), nor the size of their operations (many traded as individuals). What was causing McLoughlin to pace his fort's circular dirt path in distraction, past church, sales shop and beef, wheat and fur stores, was the fact that Americans traded liquor for furs, giving them a huge sales advantage. McLoughlin's conundrum: Should Fort Vancouver traders defy the HBC's edict and do the same?

Trading liquor for furs was an old HBC issue. Almost 150 years earlier, the liquor had been brandy. In 1682, the HBC had shipped 440 gallons of it to North America for use in trading ceremonies. Soon, bottles of brandy were extended during trade exchanges. Company directors warned employees of Fort Albany, on the west shore of James Bay, to "trade as little Brandy as possible to the Indians, we being informed it has destroyed several of them." Nevertheless, in a 1770s compendium of 16 company trade goods from brass kettles to buttons, brandy makes the list as item 10. The exchange rate was one gallon for one beaver pelt or its equivalent. Looking at the cost side of their ledgers, company accountants frowned. Genuine French brandy was too expensive for trade. Nevertheless, supplying Natives with potent drink was deemed important enough for the company to concoct an economical substitute. A few drops of iodine (or, later, molasses) gave cheap gin a nice amber hue. No iodine handy? A squirt or two of tobacco juice did the job. The HBC christened it "English brandy."

By the early 1800s, from York Factory, on Hudson Bay's western shore, to McLoughlin's Fort Vancouver on the Pacific coast, traders told tales of alcohol's devastating effect on Natives. Trader Alexander Henry the Younger told the story of a warrior who suspected his wife of infidelity. Drawing his knife in a drunken rage, he stabbed the woman repeatedly. While recovering, she plotted revenge. Made drunk again, the woman's husband was easily held down by the vengeful wife's relatives as, in Henry's words, she "applied a fire brand to his privates, and rubbed it in. She left him in a shocking condition, with the parts nearly roasted." There was no easy answer to McLoughlin's first conundrum because he and every other HBC trader faced a second problem: a man made dangerous by liquor received for his furs did not, in the end, make for a good long-term trading partner.

The peaceful merger in 1821 of the HBC with its

once-mighty rival, the North West Company—engineered, in part, by the HBC's new young governor, George Simpson—ended the Nor'Westers' reckless competition and destructive liquor exchanges. To capitalize on the change, the company instructed Simpson to ban liquor as a trade item throughout its territories within two or three years. One year later, he had reduced its use by 50 percent.

The inevitable ban extended to all forts located in Oregon Territory, a vast western wilderness owned by no nation, stretching from the Queen Charlotte Islands (now Haida Gwaii) to the border of Mexico's Spanish California. Three years after the merger, when Simpson travelled to the Columbia River Department to meet former Nor'Wester John McLoughlin, whom he had appointed as the new head of Fort Vancouver, the governor reported to London that Natives were "getting as much addicted to Drunkenness as the tribes of the East side of the Mountain." Simpson blamed traders who gave away free drams of rum; after that taste, Natives were willing to trade 10 skins for a single bottle—a much more profitable exchange than the former one skin for one gallon rate.

By 1830, McLoughlin didn't need the fort's 33-year-old counting-house clerk, James Douglas (soon to be his chief trader and second-in-command), to tell him that the company's liquor ban was costing the fort business. McLoughlin had been in the fur trade far too long not to sense what Douglas's columns of neat figures would confirm. The chief factor cautioned Simpson that American liquor was making it difficult for the HBC to compete and suggested strongly, "We must do the same or abandon the trade."

McLoughlin also reported a disturbing discovery. Using traditional culture to further their own ends, Americans were actively involved in the eons-old Native slave trade. Buying slaves from Cape Flattery Natives, traders loaded them aboard ship and then, according to McLoughlin, bartered them "to the northern tribes at about 30 beaver each, and some good-looking female slaves as high as 50." McLoughlin added, "In this inhuman traffic, they deal largely in Guns Ammunition and Liquor."

Like liquor, slavery was a "wink-and-nudge" issue for HBC men. While deploring the Native slave trade, McLoughlin turned a blind eye to slaves inside his own post. Fort Vancouver traders took Native wives who brought slaves into their white households. In London, governor and committee claimed ignorance of the situation on the Columbia until an 1836 report by the fort's Anglican chaplain revealed the practice. Parliament had sought to end the British slave trade decades before, and the HBC had no desire for the public to perceive it as a retrograde group of slavers or slave-owners. In McLoughlin's absence, it fell to James Douglas to respond, and in 1838, he admitted to "the practical evil" which "all my efforts have failed in rooting out."

Company policies formalized in London and the "practical evils" of liquor and slavery that helped make frontier lives bearable and trade profitable, including the exports of salmon and timber to Oahu, obliged McLoughlin to step nimbly and discreetly between two sets of realities. McLoughlin, managing the increasingly diversified enterprise called the Pacific depot, and Simpson, playing the trade diplomat in Europe, strategized ways to destroy their American rivals. They needn't have worried that much. As McLoughlin himself recognized, most were "mere adventurers without capital." By 1840, not even the liquor trade could save the American Fur Company or the Rocky Mountain Fur Company from their ruinous competition with one another and Fort Vancouver's direct-from-England maritime supply and provisioning system.

The collapse of the two American companies gave the HBC unhindered operations on most of the Pacific coast. The year before, in Hamburg, Simpson had managed to shut out the Boston supply trade, signing a food-for-territory agreement with the Russian American Company. In exchange for produce from the farm fields of the Pacific depot (Fort Vancouver), along with guaranteed purchases of commodities from beef to barley, the Russians offered the company a 10-year lease of 400 miles of northern coastline.

By 1842, Simpson had even convinced the Russians to halt their liquor trade. However, the HBC governor recognized that the only way to stop the practice in his own posts was to keep liquor from whites. He issued McLoughlin new orders: no sale or gift of liquor by company employees to anyone, white or Native. McLoughlin tried his best to comply, but was only partially successful.

Years before settlers' wagon trains doomed the fur trade, parties of white missionaries began to arrive. McLoughlin, who clearly saw himself as a founder of a new society as much as a fur trader, welcomed them all, much to Simpson's displeasure. The chief factor encouraged Methodist leader Jason Lee to settle in the Willamette Valley. Later, to help stem both Native and white drunkenness, he supported Lee's efforts to organize the Oregon Temperance Society.

While Simpson was in discussions with the Russians, the Boston trader *Blanche* entered the Columbia loaded with whisky. A fearful Willamette Valley missionary boarded the ship and extracted a promise from the captain that he would neither give away nor sell any liquor. The captain agreed and then did what he and his crew had been sent to do: exchange bottles for pelts with both Clatsops and Chinooks. In the night of bedlam and debauchery that followed, three Natives were shot and several more were stabbed.

McLoughlin was not blind to the bloody mayhem on his doorstep. He may have consoled himself that his men were merely handing liquor out as gifts, not selling or exchanging it in trade. If the Russians complain, he told his lieutenant, Peter Skene Ogden, tell them that the company was doing it "in consequence of its being done by the Americans." All the while, McLoughlin's heart must have ached. Two decades spent carefully nurturing an almost paternal relationship with the Natives was being undone with every bottle they emptied.

By now, liberty-loving settlers had begun to follow the missionaries' westward trail. These were committed people, so determined to live a better and freer life that they endured a harrowing trek through thousands of miles of semi-arid wilderness to do it. Not surprisingly, they quickly resented the oppressive dictates of Christian reformers and were troubled by their pervasive influence. A former New York State physician named Dr. Elijah White set about confiscating liquor and attempting to search American ships. Yet, the zealot managed to provoke the ire of missionary Lee and settlers alike by calling himself "governor" and "U.S. sub-Indian agent." It was a laughable boast, because America had no jurisdiction in the territory, but then— other than perhaps the HBC—who did? By 1843, anxious settlers had decided to found a provisional government.

When the new legislative assembly met the following year, members focused on an issue that had concerned temperate missionaries: the proliferation of makeshift illicit stills, which sometimes produced "firewater" so volatile it burst into flame. As the proposed bill's preamble reveals, wilderness legislators feared the consequences of liquor. Distilling or selling "ardent spirits" (hard liquor, not beer) would invite "swarms of the dissipated inhabitants of other Countries" and "bring upon us the swarms of savages now in our midst." Given the settlers' anxieties, the prohibition law passed easily.

There was still no law against having a drink, but liquor traffic was abolished. Fines included $50 for those caught importing booze with the intent to sell, $20 for its sale and $100 for its manufacture. With territorial law now on his side, Elijah White seized the moment. "Liquor was in our midst," he later wrote, which led to "noisy, vulgar, obscene and even diabolical expressions" by those who emptied bottles of booze.

While members of the new legislature were raising their hands in favour of the prohibition, moonshiners Richard Macray and James Conner were hard at work in the canyon below Oregon City, distilling something from "the offal of shorts [animal feed derived from the milling process], and wheat and molasses" and bottling what the locals called Blue Ruin. With ten "noble volunteers," White struck hard and fast. As the astonished moonshiners looked on, White and his group smashed their still and bottles and jugs of merchandise. Enraged, Conner challenged White to a duel. White took Conner to court instead, which fined him $500. This time, settlers could not help but applaud.

However, by the following year, with Fort Vancouver's clerks again pouring liquid gifts, previously vehement settlers merely shrugged in resignation. A new government's constitution had watered down the initial prohibition law. Now, instead of prohibiting the manufacture or sale of liquor, the government would merely regulate it. In the new Washington Territory, a referendum was held the following year on what was called "Prohibition and the Indian problem." Many voters decided that with the latter likely of diminishing concern, they could take a chance and avoid the oppressiveness of the former. Prohibition was narrowly defeated, 564 votes to 650.

Back in 1846, the Willamette Valley had passed the Licensing Act, allowing liquor's sale. An enterprising Oregon City gent, Sidney Moss, took out a $200 licence and opened the territory's first saloon, stocking it with liquor from licensed distillers. At first, Moss's only competitors were miscreants hidden away in valleys and hills, distilling up old Blue Ruin, with "much of it," Moss complained, "going to the debauched natives." Native drunks had themselves tipped Moss off as they stumbled through the muddy streets, mumbling a drinking song. The saloon proprietor was incensed enough to write down and translate the doggerel. One repeated phrase was "potlatch blue lu." Moss saw the Blue Ruin connection but likely missed the lyric's larger significance.

For generations, coastal peoples had routinely held elaborate days-long gift-giving ceremonies designed to impress visiting groups with the host chief's wealth and power. By the late 1840s, many potlatches had degenerated into what some called the "whisky feast." Visiting peoples no longer simply took away the potlatch host's gifts; they also drank them up before they stumbled back to their canoes. Excessive drinking was soon entrenched in the Natives' social culture.

By the time the regulatory liquor statutes were law, Chief

Factor McLoughlin had resigned, somewhat bitterly, from the HBC. The man the Natives called White Eagle and who was later regarded as "the father of Oregon" had moved to Oregon City, where he later operated a retail store and enjoyed a life of frontier luxury in his splendid two-storey home on the Willamette River. McLoughlin lived to see the most profound social change experienced by the two northwest American territories, and it must have saddened him deeply.

In 1855, a *Puget Sound Courier* reader had asked what citizens had to do to "rid ourselves of the mean-spirited and filthy-minded white scoundrels who cowardly deal out liquid damnation to the poor Siwashes." Five years later, nobody much cared. A series of escalating armed conflicts—the Cayuse, Coeur d'Alene and Yakama wars—had further decimated Pacific Northwest peoples as they fought white intrusions into their ancestral lands, and after gold was discovered, even into the newly established reservations the territories themselves had assigned them. Many died as they fought. Others surrendered and were executed. Some fled north across the new border to New Caledonia (later British Columbia). With the elimination of most of its customers, the once-lucrative Pacific Northwest aboriginal liquor trade all but disappeared.

However, just a few miles north of Washington Territory, McLoughlin's former chief trader was already embroiled in his own coastal whisky wars, and his battles would only intensify as the 1850s ended.

2

Opening Salvos

OH, IT WAS A GRAND FIND! Who knew exactly where it had originated; definitely not from Fort Victoria's stores, that much was certain. The likely source was one of the American schooners that had stopped on its way up the coast. But who cared? It was enough for the delighted HBC rank and file that the barrel (oh, blessed, blessed barrel!) had materialized inside the fort's palisades. Within minutes of its arrival, it was sitting inside the men's quarters with a very thirsty gang clustered about it, cups in hand.

One drink of whisky quickly followed another. It wasn't long before the cackles and howls of inebriated employees grew loud enough to be heard clearly across the fort's quadrangle and through the walls of the new governor's family quarters. James Douglas strode across the yard and knocked on the door of Chief Trader Roderick Finlayson. After a brief conversation, he and Finlayson were joined by other company officers, fort doctor John Helmcken and schoolmaster Reverend Robert Staines, the latter brandishing a sword, of all things. As the group marched across to the men's house, the inebriates inside saw them coming.

Hide it! Hide the barrel! As Finlayson and others thumped on the barred door and demanded to be let in, the drunken men frantically secreted the keg out of sight. The door was finally opened. Scowling Douglas, stern-faced Finlayson and the others pushed their way in. While the sullen employees looked on, they began to search for the hidden liquor.

Look under the floorboards! As hands began to claw at the flooring, some of the drunks brazenly stepped up and began to elbow the searchers aside. Ordering them to stand back, Finlayson and others shoved the jeering men to one end of the room. Staines walked up, pointed his sword at the group and shouted melodramatically, "Pass this who dares!" Yanking and prying, the search party pulled up the floorboards to expose the contraband keg. The drunken men were ordered out into the yard, where a sizeable gaggle of curious onlookers had gathered to watch the drama. The barrel of whisky was ceremoniously placed on end not far from the flagstaff.

Douglas glanced at his chief trader. "Knock the head out, Mr. Finlayson!" he ordered.

Finlayson nodded to clerk George Simpson, who stood

holding an axe. Simpson stepped up, swung the axe and stove in the top of the barrel, spewing its precious contents everywhere. Crying out, the company employees threw themselves on the ground, sucking up the liquor as it ran across the dirt, some scrambling on all fours to drink greedily at puddles of the stuff.

Startled by the bizarre and disgusting scene, Finlayson murmured to Helmcken, "What is to be done now?" A few minutes later, the doctor waved a small container. Tartar of emetic, he confided. The physician sprinkled the slightly poisonous substance on the rivulets and pools of whisky. Within a minute or two, the sounds of retching filled the air, and laughing onlookers watched the drunken men spew up everything they had swallowed.

An HBC man since 1819, with a wealth of trading experience in New Caledonia and at Fort Vancouver, Scotsman James Douglas was intimately familiar with the no-win Native liquor-trade situation. However, he shared Governor George Simpson's concern about white imbibing. The conduct of HBC employees had to set an example, not only for the Natives they traded with, but for other whites who supplied the company with food and materials. And a chief factor must set the best example of all. Douglas saw his priorities with a single-minded clarity; he allowed no chink in his company armour. Men saw aloofness and austerity in his deportment and heard no wit or humour in his words. "He was a very self contained man," recalled Dr. John Helmcken, the governor's future son-in-law, "rarely giving his confidence to anyone and to me scarcely ever, he considering me to be a 'radical'; his abhorrence."

Writer Matthew Macfie, who arrived in the colonies in 1860, was unsympathetic about this "dignified old fur trapper." Douglas's "efforts to appear grand and even august were ludicrously out of proportion to the insignificant population he governed." Macfie reported that when Douglas routinely appeared in this small frontier town in semi-military uniform, "the temptation of local wits [likely American] to satirise so preposterous a spectacle was irresistible."

No one could dispute that the fort on the southern tip of Vancouver Island belonged to Douglas. In 1842, he had helped the company choose its location, stating, "It lies about half a mile off the main strait of De Fuca, in a snug sheltered cove . . . accessible at all seasons to vessels which may anchor within 50 feet of the bank on which the Fort will stand." Within months, he was at the site, instructing "6 men to dig a well and 6 others to square building timbers" while contracting with Songhees Natives to procure pickets, paying "a blanket for every forty . . . which they bring."

This new post was critical to the company; it meant more than avoiding the treacherous shipwrecking sandbars at the mouth of the Columbia, more than simply securing northern fur-trade business. Simpson, McLoughlin and Douglas realized the US would soon lay claim to Oregon Territory. Fort Langley had been established on what was called Frazer's River to thwart potential intrusion of American traders. Now, Douglas's Fort Victoria would help thwart American expansionism.

When Douglas arrived at the fort as chief factor in 1849, the British government had rented the entire island to the company for seven shillings a year. The HBC promised to bring out settlers and develop the Colony of Vancouver Island. A colony needed a governor, and the one chosen was an obscure barrister named Richard Blanshard. Blanshard, in ill health and hopelessly outmatched by the experienced Douglas, lasted less than two years. When he left, London replaced him with Douglas himself. Douglas bore the double mantle of chief factor and governor with inner stoicism and outward dignity.

However, as governor and colonists could attest, there was absolutely nothing dignified about a stumbling drunk. By 1853, there was no lack of, as Douglas put it, "scandalous scenes of drunkenness and excess" around the fort. Every night, dozens of inebriates staggered out of the new waterfront saloon, Ship Inn, operated by James Yates. Yates was making far more money than he ever had as a former HBC ships' carpenter; it wouldn't be long before others emulated him. Meanwhile, the colony needed revenue with which to build much-needed roads, bridges and schools. Douglas decided to remedy one problem through control of the other. He would license liquor vendors, and, not surprisingly, made the HBC the colony's liquor wholesaler.

When Douglas proposed his licensing policy to members of the colony's council, it took a day-long debate around the table to convince the other two men to agree. Douglas had conspired to hold the meeting when he knew it was unlikely that the third councillor, Captain James Cooper—a friend of Yates already dabbling in the liquor business—could attend. The governor carefully timed the delivery of his notice of the meeting after Cooper had left for distant Metchosin. While Douglas drove home the point that licensing was the "best means of restraining the abuse, and excessive importation of spirituous liquors into this Colony," in the end, it was likely the need for revenue that swayed the two council members. Tellingly, one of Douglas's edicts was that no member of council could involve himself in the liquor trade.

When he got the news of the meeting and resulting liquor-licence policy, Cooper was outraged. He drew up a list of grievances against Douglas and got Yates to do the same. Cooper also enlisted the support of Robert Staines, the pretentious chaplain and schoolmaster, to vouch for the authenticity of the grievances of the growing anti-Douglas faction, and sent the documents off to the colonial secretary in London. Douglas could not have been surprised at the Anglican clergyman's antipathy. Staines, Douglas noted, "entertains a most unaccountable and unreasonable dislike to the Company, and has done so ever since his arrival in this country."

All of this might account for Douglas's uncharacteristically impassioned defence of his licence policy in his next dispatches. The vendor licences, he told his superiors, were "fiercely opposed by the whole body of publicans and other blood suckers, who are preying upon the vitals of the Colony, exhausting its wealth and making a return of poisonous drinks, ruinous to the morals of the people, and the prolific source of poverty and crime."

The issue for "publicans and other blood suckers" wasn't the cost of a licence. James Yates could afford the initial annual fee that his competitors would also willingly pay. What Yates and Cooper more vehemently opposed was Douglas's autocratic assault on the principle of free enterprise. To Douglas's dismay, increasingly vocal opposition proved to be the spark that kindled the fires of reform. Three years later, while still "utterly averse to universal suffrage," Douglas acceded to the wishes of the British government and prepared the colony for its first election. Although the assembly was a mere consultative body and the governor held veto power, the liquor wars had done their part to bring democracy of a sort to the young colony.

In London, HBC committeemen and government officials undoubtedly appreciated Douglas's firm hand in maintaining control over the tiny colony on the outer reaches of the British Empire. In his licensing report, Douglas told them what they wanted to hear, but he knew better. Liquor had become a part of everyday life for almost every white person (meaning men) in the island colony, as it had in the American coastal territories. He admitted as much when he wrote, "I do not suppose that the duty will put a stop to drunkenness." How right he was.

The forbidding wilderness, and the unending toil it cost colonists to wrest farms from it, gave liquor—port, cider, ale and whisky—a special importance in Fort Victoria society. In 1854, Christmas merrymaking emptied so many bottles and jugs, there was nothing left for celebrating the New Year, "a day above all days, for rioting in drunkenness," moaned newcomer Robert Melrose. Engaged in five years of backbreaking servitude on the HBC's Craigflower Farm, Melrose liked (and likely needed) a drink as much as the next man, which was very much indeed.

"Then, what are we to expect," Melrose noted in his diary, "of this young, but desperate Colony of ours where dissipation is carried on to such extremities . . . but one drunk and another drunk and so on. The grog-shops were drained of every sort of liquor, not a drop to be got for either love or money." Melrose thought "it would almost take a line of packet ships, running regular between here and San Francisco, to supply this Island with grog, so great a thirst prevails amongst its inhabitants." Any occasion—the start of horse-racing season at Beacon Hill Park, for example—was a good excuse to open bottles and raise glasses. "The author, half-drunk," Melrose admitted in another diary entry. As his diary makes clear, he was not alone: "James Downie, ½ drunk . . . D. Veitch, ¾ D. . . . Enoch Morris, ¾ D."

Of course, men of the highest rank loved drink just as much as men of the lowest. That number included Matthew Baillie Begbie, the colony's first judge. Begbie arrived from London just a few months after gold had been discovered on the Fraser River. He served as county court judge for the mainland colony. Almost a year later, accompanied by registrar Arthur Bushby, Begbie set out on a circuit of the "goldfields," as they were invariably called, with instructions to report back to Governor Douglas on the state of the country and hold court, if necessary. He did so at Fort Langley, New Westminster and the gold-rush drinking and gambling shantytown called Yale.

What an adventure for the young former barrister from London! In the words of Arthur Bushby, it was all "glorious fun." Bushby wasn't referring to the canoeing and riding. When the day's travelling was done and the party was sitting around a riverside campfire, one and all soon became, in Bushby's words, "drunk, drunk, drunk." As Begbie's party approached Yale, the judge and his companions likely remained unaware of the special efforts prospectors had taken the year before to prohibit the same alcoholic beverages the judge and his party were enjoying.

It happened on March 23. Decades later, the date still came easily to James Moore, because it was his birthday. Moore turned 26 on that day in 1858, but he had another far more important reason—a history-making reason—to celebrate the date. On Moore's birthday, his small party made the first gold strike on the lower Fraser River. Young James Moore was among the first of an eventual 30,000 American gold-seekers who made their way north to seek their fortune.

In February of that year, an initial gold shipment from Fort Victoria had arrived at the former gold-rush city of San Francisco. Unloaded from the *Otter* into a wagon, the boxes of gold nuggets and dust were escorted up the slope to the US Mint for smelting. The gold's arrival electrified the city's former and potential prospectors, who had almost given up hopes of a new bonanza. Was this it? A few nights later, Moore and others were puffing cigars, pouring drinks and dealing cards inside the city's Number 3 Engine House and asking each other the same question.

Through the swirl of smoke, Moore saw one gentleman wearing a knowing smile. He was Charles H. Hempstead, superintendent of the US Mint's San Francisco operation, a man with "inside information," and happy to share it. What struck him most, Hempstead told the hushed group, was the exceptional quality of the gold. "Boys," he assured them all, "the next excitement will be to the Fraser River." That was an interesting comment, because Hempstead likely knew the gold in Douglas's shipment hadn't been found on the Fraser; it had been discovered hundreds of miles northeast, on the Thompson River. Every man in the room realized that the safest travel to the Thompson wasn't hiking through territories aflame with Native uprisings but sailing up the coast and then (they guessed) following the Fraser inland. Within weeks, Moore and 14 others were steaming north.

After stops at Forts Langley and Hope (where the HBC trader's comments confirmed that the group had beaten everyone else to the Fraser), they continued up the river. That day—Moore's birthday—they stopped for lunch on a large gravel bar. While others ate and drank, a restless fellow named Hill walked with his gold pan over to the mossy rocks by the water's edge and made a discovery that rivalled the earlier one made by the carpenter building Sutter's sawmill on the American River. The result of that find was the California gold rush of '49. Eleven years later, Hill's discovery would have the same effect. The group's travels had ended. Their problems, however, were just beginning.

On the gravel soon christened "Hill's Bar," the first problem wasn't finding gold (every man was soon digging out hundreds of dollars' worth), it was finding food. Unprepared for long-term American visitors, Fort Langley didn't have a large stock of provisions; the foraging party returned with only limited supplies. The second problem was that there were now more people on the bar. About 300 curious Natives—men, women and children—had come down the river, camped out and started digging for gold, too. Work continued peacefully for a few weeks, until, Moore recalled, "we noticed a boat coming up the river loaded." The men were elated—food at last! However, as Moore relates, the boat's cargo held "not a pound of provisions for sale," but instead "nothing but liquor." Liquor proved to be their biggest problem yet.

The boat's owner, a whisky peddler by the name of Taylor, quickly discovered "the Indians all had gold dust." That suited Taylor; they were better-paying customers than savvy prospectors. Sales opened at five dollars a bottle, payable in dust. "The Indians not knowing its value, allowed Taylor to help himself, which he did." The alarmed prospectors held a quick meeting and then approached Taylor and offered to buy up his whole cargo at a wholesale price. Taylor merely laughed them off. "That night," Moore remembered, "the Indians all got drunk and howled all night on the bar."

The next day, the prospectors took action. "We marched down to Taylor's camp and confiscated the whole contents of his cargo of liquor, got axes and smashed in the heads of each keg of liquor and dumped the contents on the bar, and gave Taylor twenty minutes to strike his camp and leave, which he did in less than the time allotted. This," Moore concluded proudly but incorrectly, "was the first prohibition act put into force without delay in British Columbia."

Governor Blanshard and his successor, James Douglas, had had little difficulty making the same prohibition decisions as Hill's Bar prospectors. As chief factor, Douglas had watched Blanshard sign an 1850 proclamation to prohibit "the free and unrestricted traffic in spirituous liquors" to both whites and Natives, not only around Fort Victoria, but up the coast as well. The imbibing of Fort Rupert miners and labourers was a concern, as it likely made the men less industrious and efficient at their jobs, but the real threat, the governor noted, was the potential effect of liquor on "the numerous, savage, and treacherous" Natives nearby.

Four years later, in 1854, fear of liquor-provoked uprisings motivated the island colony's council to pass new legislation: "An Act prohibiting the Gift or Sale of Intoxicating Liquors to the Indians." While the formal rationale for the law noted that liquor was "manifestly injurious to the Native Tribes," the more important reason for its passage was the perception that intoxicated Natives were "endangering the public peace and the lives and property of Her Majesty's subjects." Douglas took pains to reinforce that danger in his inaugural address to the colony's new legislative assembly. While acknowledging that "the friendship of the natives is at all times useful," Douglas reminded Speaker John Helmcken and the six newly elected legislators—saloonkeeper James Yates among them—that "their enmity may become more disastrous than any other calamity to which the colony is directly exposed." Yates had more to lose than most colonists, as he already enjoyed hundreds of acres of landholdings near the fort. It was little wonder that before long he was assisting others in apprehending whisky traders in the area.

Just a few months after Jim Moore and his buddies

smashed Taylor's whisky kegs on Hill's Bar, Douglas issued another prohibition proclamation while visiting Fort Hope, in hopes of averting a "calamity" on the mainland. Those caught selling liquor to Natives would be fined. Somehow, the threat of a fine didn't have the same sting as pouring whisky onto the gravel. Colonial governors were good at making prohibition laws, but unlike Moore and his miner companions, they had no way to enforce them, as Moore put it, "without delay." And that, as the colonies' prohibitionists soon realized, was a critical difference.

Some missionaries had been sent out to save colonists' souls, most others to save Native ones. There was no hope of saving the souls of either if their owners were insensible from drink. Four Wesleyan Methodists from Ontario were among the first to arrive at Fort Victoria, and in their island and mainland congregations, they preached the complete elimination of alcohol. Reverend Lampfrit, an Oblate father living up-island with the Cowichan, was undoubtedly doing the same. By the 1860s, Anglican, Presbyterian and Roman Catholic churches were all well represented in the two colonies, both in urban centres and throughout the frontier.

When he visited Native villages in his mainland diocese, Roman Catholic bishop Louis-Joseph d'Herbomez held out the promise of a permanent priest if Natives pledged to live their lives in an appropriate manner. Kneeling before the bishop, Natives solemnly renounced polygamy, gambling and liquor. In return, each village was given a flag emblazoned with three words that neatly summed up both the way to redemption and the church's frontier objectives: Religion, Temperance, Civilization.

In 1859, the American prohibition society Sons of Temperance opened a Fort Victoria chapter. This was a force to be reckoned with—south of the border, 5,000 chapters of the organization flourished. The group's thousands of members called each other "brother," and the society's secret rites, handshake and password were only revealed upon payment of a two-dollar initiation fee, which was a hefty sum at the time, roughly equivalent to a workingman's weekly wages.

The Dashaway Association of Victoria was more moderate. What members "dashed away" from was, in the parlance of the time, "the flowing bowl." Amor De Cosmos, the flamboyant and outspoken editor of the *British Colonist*, became a charter member and the association's printer, publishing its 1860 constitution and bylaws. His commercial connection calls into question his true commitment to the cause. However, for De Cosmos, who liked a drink as much as the next man, Dashaway membership would have been a relatively painless cost of doing business. Permanent abstinence wasn't even part of the Dashaway creed. Members merely signed a pledge to abstain for a period of 6 to 12 months. Those who fell off the (water) wagon were simply given a reprimand for their first offence and a five-dollar fine for every tumble thereafter.

Outside the towns, whisky's ravages among the Native peoples continued unabated. By early 1860, most colonists may have become inured to it, but newcomers were dismayed by what they saw. One who was perhaps more sensitive than most to the Natives' plight was Anglican bishop George Hills. Arriving at Fort Victoria, he quickly noted that "more than half the Songhee are destroyed, principally from drink." Hills set out to explore the north part of the island. Somewhere between the fort and the coal town of Nanaimo, he witnessed a shocking sight.

"Passed a village of Northern Indians," the Bishop wrote in his diary. "There was a frightful scene of drunken confusion. The poor creatures were running about like crazy people in a lunatic yard . . . rolling and tumbling one against the other." He was duly informed that not all Natives were besotted by booze. Other tribesmen took action against the drunkards in their midst, who were "bound hand and foot, tethered to a stump or tree. This is common practice [for] . . . the poor Indian [who] when under the influence of drink is a menace."

Anglican missionaries and clergymen saw the navy as the solution to the problem of Native drunkenness and urged the governor to use gunboats and Jack tars to enforce the colonies' legislation. The suggestion likely raised some eyebrows; not long before, Her Majesty's Royal Navy had been perceived as part of the problem, not a solution.

CHAPTER

3

Prohibition's Enforcers

WHEN HMS *THETIS* ARRIVED AT Esquimalt in the spring of 1852, it was Vancouver Island's wilderness that first made an indelible impression on Gunnery Lieutenant John Moresby: "Trees, trees everywhere, many of them 200 feet high, laced with undergrowth, hoary with lichen." Once the 36-gun frigate reached the Queen Charlotte Islands—where Douglas had dispatched it to investigate reports of gold—officers and crew began to trade with the island Natives. There, Lieutenant Moresby witnessed a much less bucolic sight. "It is sad to think that these fine people, degraded by contact with so-called civilization, have almost disappeared," he wrote almost a half-century later. "Indeed, the beginnings could be seen on our own quarter-deck as they exchanged their furs for 'fire-water' and drank it greedily."

On a visit to the north coast the following year, a small paddlewheel sloop of six guns, HMS *Virago*, visited Fort Simpson, a major HBC trading centre near today's Prince Rupert. According to the ship's diary-keeping surgeon, Henry Travan, officers got quickly to work, invited Tsimshian people aboard and bartered marten and bear skins for rum. When the sloop anchored in Esquimalt, the captain, Commander James Prevost, granted the crew shore leave. The sailors weren't long at the fort before some of them found— in Travan's words—"some strong Yankee Stuff which made them very tipsy." Fights broke out constantly, "terrifying the Indians and keeping Hudson's Bay Company people in constant alarm." Not all the crew made it back to the ship that night. As darkness fell, inebriated sailors stumbled off the narrow trail running between the fort and Esquimalt harbour, becoming hopelessly lost in the forest. They thrashed around in the underbrush until morning, when some Songhees found them and led them back to the trail.

The episode alluded to another reason crewmen were eager to hike the trail between Esquimalt harbour and what would later become the town of Victoria: Native women. Matthew Macfie reported that along the route, "the extent the nefarious practices [sexual favours] . . . are encouraged by the crews of Her Majesty's ships is a disgrace to the service they represent, and a scandal to the country."

The man responsible for these wandering drunks, the *Virago*'s captain—in a twist of irony—was one of the most devout coastal commanders. By 1857, James Prevost had a new, larger ship (the screw corvette HMS *Satellite*) and a new mission: to survey the exact position of the 49th parallel. Before leaving England, Prevost—convinced only Christianity could save the coastal Natives—had persuaded the Admiralty to allow him to bring out a young member of the Church Missionary Society. The accordion-playing young Anglican, William Duncan, was destined to become the most successful missionary on the Pacific coast.

A few months later, James Douglas was reporting to British authorities that American gold-seekers were "crowding into the British possessions with reckless precipitation." Send more warships, Douglas begged the Admiralty. Rear Admiral Robert L. Baynes, commander-in-chief, Pacific station, thought he should see this phenomenon for himself and was aboard his 84-gun flagship, HMS *Ganges*, when she dropped anchor in Esquimalt in early October 1858. He was there again in 1860, during an outbreak of Native violence within sight of the fort's bastions.

On orders from the Haida chieftain who owned him, a slave had killed a chief of the north-coast Tlingit people who was visiting Fort Victoria. To avoid more tribal bloodshed, Douglas ordered the Haida moved away from the other groups. Tension mounted when the incensed Haida took potshots from shore at the schooner *Royal Charlie* as she entered the Inner Harbour. The angry Haida may have had good reason to take aim at the schooner: she was a north-coast whisky vessel. At Douglas's request, Baynes had ship's boats block the harbour entrance and ordered crews to search canoes for weapons. *Ganges* marines marched over to the Haida camp and confiscated muskets, knives and revolvers. Tlingit leaders took the governor's advice to seek British justice instead of their traditional bloody revenge. A deputation visited the police station and lodged a complaint.

Two warrants were issued, and a Haida chief and his brother were duly arrested. Just as a jailer was about to search his prisoners, the pair pulled concealed knives and attacked him. Policemen came to the rescue (one, throwing himself across the jailer's torso, probably saved his life), and when the shouting and shooting ended, both Haida lay dead. Rear Admiral Baynes had seen enough and decided to share his own thoughts on the matter with the Admiralty.

In Bayne's mind, it wasn't simply inter-tribal enmity that caused the recent bloodshed in Fort Victoria, it was booze. It was very easy for Natives to purchase liquor around the fort, Baynes informed officials by letter. The liquor traffic was extensive and, he claimed, the governor reluctant to act—or, at least, to undertake the necessary expense to do so. Baynes then decided to let himself and the Admiralty off the hook by suggesting that chasing white whisky traders was beyond the navy's jurisdiction.

The traders appeared beyond the reach of the newly established police forces, as well. Chartres Brew, a former member of the Royal Irish Constabulary, had been sent out by London to organize law enforcement in mainland gold camps. After taking stock of the situation, Brew informed the governor that the job would take 250 police at Fort Hope, another 350 at Yale and another 250 at the newly constructed Fort Dallas at the fork of the Thompson and Fraser Rivers. To support this force, he suggested "three or four" police gunboats to patrol the Fraser itself. Two years later, Brew's police force was so woefully undermanned that some road work in New Westminster was cancelled because there weren't enough officers available to supervise the chain gang ordered to do the improvements. Whisky traders throughout BC scoffed. In spite of all the rhetoric—and various legislation and proclamations—business boomed.

Victoria's police force, organized just a few months before Brew's arrival, fared little better. One exception in 1861 was due to the stealth of four Native officers. They had been watching a certain John Wemyss for a while; some Songhees had been buying his liquor wares often enough to provoke angry complaints, but Police Commissioner Augustus Pemberton had instructed officers that they had to catch the whisky peddler in the act before laying charges and bringing him to trial. The four decided to engineer a sting operation, enlisting the aid of two "klootchmen" (Native women) to pose as thirsty customers.

The women were instructed to visit the ravine where Wemyss's hovel was located, knock on his door, ask for a couple of bottles and show him money. The concealed officers were watching when Wemyss snatched the payment and thrust bottles in the women's hands. They sprang into action, beat on the door with their truncheons and hauled Wemyss out. The police escort didn't get too far before news of the apprehension spread and vengeful Natives lined their route. "Bravo! Indian Policemen," the *Colonist* crowed the next day. The newspaper reported that by the time the four proud officers reached the Bastion Street jail, their prisoner "was about the worst-used specimen of humanity that has ever been taken to jail in this town."

However, by 1863, it was obvious that the tiny police force of the recently incorporated city had no hope of discouraging, let alone halting, whisky sales to local Natives. Trading continued, despite weekly arraignments of whisky sellers in stipendiary magistrate Augustus Pemberton's police court. Charges were often dismissed due to lack of evidence.

One prohibition enforcement statistic appears impressive: 336 individuals were arrested for selling liquor to Natives in and around Victoria. However, this number does not represent arrests made in a single year, but rather throughout a period of seven years, ending in 1864. At a time when Native drinking was a leading social and law-enforcement problem around the city, this small number of arrests is almost laughable. The actual number of convictions was even smaller: just 240. One-third of those brought before magistrates during this long period of civic history got off scot-free.

Cynical colonists might have wondered just how many liquor sellers managed to evade arrest altogether during those long, thirsty years. The success rate of the Victoria police in apprehending liquor traders could not have been very high; arresting liquor traders was just one of many duties of the very small number of policemen patrolling essentially the same area as today's force does, but doing so on foot, without the benefit of mechanized vehicles and electronic communications. Erring on the side of caution, if the number of arrests was a conservative 30 percent of the total number of traders actively intoxicating local Natives (those arrested including a number of repeat offenders), it means there were close to a thousand locals toiling in the illicit sector, a number representing a startling 15 percent of the city's 1864 population!

From the thirsty Natives' perspective, the problem with whisky traders was they always wanted something in return for the bottle. To avoid the time and effort of trapping and skinning animals, enterprising coastal tribesmen started to make booze themselves. Usually, their product was simply a fermented mixture of molasses, flour, berries, potatoes, yeast and water. Some went further and actually distilled the liquid using old oil cans for retorts and kelp scooped from the beaches as "organic" condensing tubes. The result was known as hoochinoo, or "hooch," a name often used for homemade liquor today.

As stomach-churning as hooch sounds, it was probably far more palatable—and healthful—than the product whisky traders were foisting off on their Native customers. In one of his 1866 dispatches to London, Vancouver Island governor Arthur Kennedy shared the not-so-secret ingredients of the traders' evil concoction with the Colonial Secretary: "The alcohol is generally diluted with salt water, and flavoured to suit the Indian taste either as brandy, rum or whiskey, camphine, creosote, and even sulphuric acid being (I am credibly informed) used to give strength and flavour." Many drinkers didn't die a slow death due to alcoholism; they died a quick death by poisoning.

The growing manufacture of hooch may have been one reason legislators began to wonder about the practicality of Native prohibition and its enforcement. However, a larger issue led a growing number to question the war against whisky traders. Apprehending, charging, trying and imprisoning traders cost the colony money. Moreover, law enforcement was economically counterproductive. Why outlaw the sale of booze to Natives if the colony needed revenue from liquor sales? Why not legalize liquor sales to Natives? The reason was that the fear of drunken Natives proved more compelling than nervousness over potential revenue shortfalls. In its 1860–61 session, the House of Assembly passed the Indian Liquor Act of 1860. The bill had been introduced by member Alfred Waddington, a prosperous old windmill tilter who owned dozens of downtown Victoria lots and leased businesses that lined both sides of the little street still known today as Waddington Alley.

A successful man of commerce, Waddington was also a man of some conscience. So, evidently, in this instance, were most of his fellow legislators. Unlike the acrimonious bill on liquor taxation, Waddington's bill ("For better Prohibiting the Sale or Gift of Intoxicating Drinks to the Indians") barely caused a ripple of dissent in the House. On November 2, 1860, it replaced Governor Douglas's 1854 Act of Council. The town's liquor men did not share Waddington's sense of conscience about what the *Daily British Colonist* called "the sale of delightful poison to the Siwashes," but despite their efforts to overturn Waddington's Indian Liquor Act, it remained in force.

By this time, Alfred Waddington was already obsessed with a potential Bute Inlet shortcut to the Cariboo gold creeks. It was through this doomed endeavour that Waddington became a north-coast prohibitionist. In the spring of 1863, "Old Waddy" and his crew steamed up to Bute Inlet—the start of the proposed road—to begin their work season. They found hundreds of Homalco, Eucletaw and Klahoose people and even some of their traditional enemies, the Tsilhqot'in, crowding the mouth of the Homathko River. Near starvation, they had wintered together, hoping for work and food when Waddington (whom the Natives called the "White Tyhee" or chief) and his "King George Men" returned. Waddington made another discovery a few nights later: "A number of our Indians were raving mad with drink," he later informed *Colonist* readers, and "I was determined to put a stop to this."

As the Homalco capered about, Waddington and 10 others paddled down the inlet and spotted a small, single-masted craft silhouetted against the horizon. Waddington's men confiscated a half-empty 10-gallon keg of something resembling liquor, pouring it into the water. Waddington ordered the trader out of the area, warning that if his boat was seen again, it would be confiscated. Taking down Waddington's name and that of his foreman, the angry trader threatened lawsuits. Waddington laughed him off.

As usual, not all the Natives imbibed. Some were as frightened as the whites, but for a different reason: they had to bear the brunt of beatings and injury from their own drunken brothers, sons and husbands. Waddington likely concluded that the trader wouldn't be suing anyone if the Homalco he had been poisoning caught up with him. The trader disappeared. However, Waddington's forthright action was more than an act of benevolence.

Waddington feared drunken Natives camped out near his work site would endanger his crew. Moreover, drunken men did not make good workers, and before the season was out, Waddington would hire some of these men as packers. However, there was likely another strategy at work, and in this respect (although not in others) the entrepreneur was no fool. In Waddington's hands, the episode became a wonderful public-relations opportunity, aimed not only at the potential investors he attempted to attract through his letters to the *Colonist*, but also directly at inlet Natives. Word of "old Waddy's" bravery against the trader spread quickly through Native families, as it had the year before when he had avoided potential inter-tribal violence by successfully interceding in an abduction, bartering for the return of a chief's daughter. All the Natives respected the White Tyhee for his actions on their behalf, and relations remained peaceful—at least until the following work season.

As for wider Native prohibition enforcement—Rear Admiral Baynes's opinion notwithstanding—many colonists expected the navy to do battle against whisky peddlers. Unfortunately, the navy didn't have the ships or men to fight this particular conflict as extensively as most residents wished. The navy had other wars to wage, against slavery, piracy and settlers' deaths at Natives' hands, and also was charged with attempting to keep British colonial sovereignty intact during the onslaught of armed American gold-seekers. Governor Douglas was, therefore, forced to "pick his battles" in the war against whisky traders.

The battles he chose for the navy concerned liquor traffic in the Inner Passage near the coal port of Nanaimo, at Port Simpson, the mostly Native settlement that had grown around Fort Simpson, and on Dundas Island, just south of the Alaska Panhandle. In September 1862, the paddle-sloop *Devastation* sailed up the coast with New Westminster's harbour master and a BC colonial agent on board. The ship's commander, John W. Pike, also took with him a schooner skipper's complaint of Indian attack. The skipper wanted justice, but Pike wasn't so sure that justice hadn't already been served.

At Nass Bay, the schooner *Nonpareil* had been trading with the Nisga'a, exchanging pure alcohol and a lamp fluid called camphene, derived from distilled turpentine, neither "uncommon articles of trade," according to Pike. The rate of exchange was half a pint for a mink skin and a quarter of a gallon for a marten or bear. What made whisky trading a risky business was the fact that one's customers were likely to become drunk and unpredictable. Crewmen sometimes became unpredictable, too, eager to take advantage of customers in drunken stupors—especially if the customers had winsome wives. This time, to make matters worse, the covetous crewman was Tsimshian, no friend of the Nisga'a.

Some time previously, Tsimshian and Nisga'a almost came to blows over a local chief's wife. Instead of violence, the Nisga'a opted for theft and ransacked the boat. Perhaps against his better judgment, given the potentially lethal nature of the "trade goods," Commander Pike carefully explained to the Nisga'a that they had no right to steal, and the Nisga'a made efforts to return the property they had seized.

Nearing Dundas Island, *Devastation* intercepted the well-known New Westminster whisky schooner *Hamley*. Pike put the harbour master and colonial agent aboard. When the schooner's captain couldn't produce a permit, manifest or bill of lading, Pike ordered his men to dump the 300-gallon cargo, including 14 five-gallon tins of pure alcohol, into the sea.

The following year, 1863, Commander Pike made special efforts to curtail the heinous trade in misery and death. *Devastation* visited Hornby Island, a well-known whisky traders' rendezvous. There, Pike seized the liquid cargo of a wrecked schooner, *Explorer*, intended for Native trade on the Stikine River in defiance of Britain's treaty with Russia. The commander impounded the cargo and leased a sloop to take it down to New Westminster customs officers. Near Fort Rupert, Pike detained vessels, interrogated traders and seized hundreds of gallons of liquor. On Portland Canal, *Devastation* seized three vessels, one of which, *Langley*, was a floating distillery. The price of *Langley*'s booze was high; it was costing the Natives everything of value. Pike impounded *Langley* and towed her and two other ships to New Westminster.

Their boats tied up on the Fraser River wharves, the skippers faced the wrath of Chartres Brew, who sat in judgment and heard heart-rending testimony from a northern Native. Two captains were charged $500 each and lost both their vessels and their cargoes. Some proceeds of their sales lined the pockets of *Devastation*'s officers and crew. Most of the confiscated ships had been outward bound from Victoria. Like many in New Westminster, Brew was no friend of the neighbouring colony. He commented sardonically that if the navy's successes continued, British Columbia would soon have all the shipping in Victoria tied up as prizes on the Fraser River.

For once, Victoria's *British Colonist* ignored the typical New Westminster jibe. Instead, editor Amor De Cosmos pondered what it would take to stop coastal whisky trading once and for all. In a lengthy editorial titled "Repression of Illicit Trade," the editor's heartfelt musing was rich in rhetoric but lacked concrete suggestions, only sighing that the "present laws are altogether too mild." The column likely reflected the public's preoccupation and frustration with the potentially disastrous trade. Liquor posed a danger to the Natives themselves, to be sure: "The native witness [in Justice Brew's courtroom] the other day, when describing in his own tongue the terrible scourge the white men had brought among them, only echoed the sentiments of his race." However, the editor's real concern was that every exchange or sale a whisky trader made was "endangering the safety of white settlers."

In light of what should have been a heartening courtroom conclusion arising out of the *Devastation* case, editor Amor De Cosmos instead offered little hope that legally imposed penalties would discourage the liquor trade. "What do men making such enormous profits—men backed up by wealthy merchants—care for a fine of a few hundred dollars, or the confiscation of their vessel?" De Cosmos asked, clearly referring to Brew's judgment. "Why, such a punishment is a mere nothing to them."

As De Cosmos implied, illicit north-coast trade was supplied by Victoria liquor dealers located on Government, Yates and Wharf streets. Many retailers and saloon owners (some representing San Francisco wholesalers) were cloaked in the guise of respected business professionals and evaded the law's scrutiny. All this made the navy's victories over the whisky trade appear a trifle hollow.

In Victoria, at a time when thousands of visiting Natives camped out in Roderick Finlayson's nearby farm fields, fear of a Native-white war sparked by the liquor trade was almost palpable. Exactly two years before De Cosmos's editorial appeared, traders aboard *Laurel*, coasting just off the Saanich Peninsula, decided to stretch one keg of whisky into two with the addition of seawater. After sampling their enhanced whisky, outraged Haida customers paddled back to the schooner and stripped her of everything they could throw into their large canoes. Reaching Fort Victoria, the traders demanded retribution. At the governor's suggestion to the rear admiral—for the Haida's behaviour could not go unpunished—HMS *Forward* steamed away to bring the culprits to justice.

The gunboat located the Haida just south of Campbell River. A Nanaimo magistrate and an HBC interpreter nervously agreed to meet with 300 affronted Haida. The two barely managed to escape back to the ship. The Haida dug in as *Forward*'s cannons fired some high warning shots. The Haida peppered the gunboat with musket fire. *Forward*'s gunners lowered their sights. Broadsides blasted canoes to kindling, shattered trees and destroyed the Natives' log barricades. While Lieutenant-Commander Charles Robson's intent was "to destroy in preference to an indiscriminate slaughter," two chiefs died and warriors were wounded. Five Haida leaders were arrested and charged with piracy.

While the Haida awaited their trial in Victoria's jail, investigations were launched. When the traders' nefarious whisky salting came to light, sympathies were aroused and the Haida prisoners were set free. The traders were deemed to have got what they deserved. The governor wrote that the "Hyder Indians," as he called them, "who fired upon and insulted Her Majesty's flag" got what they deserved, too. "The punishment inflicted upon them was the result of their own rashness and was merited and necessary."

In 1866, a man of God and advocate of Native self-respect through self-sufficiency became one of the staunchest enforcers of Aboriginal prohibition. The steam corvette *Clio* had apprehended a number of whisky traders near Kitimat. Tsimshian-speaking William Duncan—the same missionary brought out by Christian commander James Prevost nine years earlier—clambered up on board *Clio* to try the suspects.

In the intervening years, Duncan appeared, at least to many visiting churchmen, to have done wonders with the Natives. He operated Metlakatla Christian Mission near today's Prince Rupert, and later, the second Metlakatla village in Alaska, a one-of-a-kind self-sustaining West Coast community complete with a commercial sawmill and various cottage industries, all operated by coastal Natives. When he heard the evidence against the traders, the man who admonished villagers "to cease drinking intoxicating liquor" (number 6 in the formal list of 15 village rules) regarded the accused as agents of the devil's temptation. His sentence stunned the prisoners and made a mockery of Brew's earlier punishments. Three captains each received fines of £600 to £800 (roughly US$3,500 to $4,000). The captains vowed to appeal the incredibly harsh sentences and did so once they reached Victoria. All verdicts were quashed and the fines cancelled.

Despite occasional headline-making successes, such as in 1865 and 1866, when *Clio* impounded three whisky schooners in the vicinity of Port Simpson, periodic cruises by navy ships could not stem the relentless tide of liquor that inundated coastal Natives. In the war against Native liquor, both civic and colonial governments went down to largely unadmitted defeat. More obviously defeated were the Native peoples further decimated by the traders' liquid wares.

4

Ironies of War

ADMITTEDLY, HE WAS OUTNUMBERED four-to-one, but Victoria police sergeant George Blake may have thought that unexpectedly getting the drop on the quartet of Songhees at gunpoint would be enough to convince them to surrender meekly. He would then escort them into town to the Bastion Street jail. Blake certainly wasn't going to leave evidence behind, just a short walk from the long, low Songhees houses that hugged the nearby beach. His prisoners could carry the confiscated 10-gallon cans of alcohol.

However, the Natives were standing in their new reserve, which gave them, at least psychologically, a home-territory advantage and infused them with more courage than Blake expected. The thought of losing all that precious alcohol likely gave them a sense of desperation. Besides, the odds were in their favour. Within moments of stepping out of the brush, Blake was fighting for his life. Damn that Charlie Brown!

In the records of Fort Victoria's war on the Native whisky trade, no one matches whisky seller Charles Brown for tenacity, stubbornness, unethical business dealings and repeated jail terms. To this day, nobody is sure whether Brown's long arrest record was the result of bad luck, bad timing, bad judgment or a combination of all three. Like the story of John Wemyss, the saga of Charlie Brown has its lighter moments, but the eventual fate of this whisky seller was certainly no laughing matter.

Charlie Brown was first arrested for selling liquor to Natives around Fort Victoria in 1859. It earned him a sentence of hard labour. Clothed in the colonial prisoner's garb of moleskin pants, red checkered shirt and blue cloth cap, he was put to work, leg irons clanking, tamping down rock to harden the surface of the fort's primitive streets. Over the next two years, Brown was back in Bastion Street's jail repeatedly on alcohol-related offences.

Brown's second prison term was earned, ironically, for *not* supplying liquor to a Native. Brown took $20 of the thirsty man's money but never delivered the goods. The disappointed customer sought redress, and Brown was found guilty of swindling. A further stint in what the locals called the "Hotel de Pemberton," resulted from his sale of 10 gallons of alcohol to a Native woman, a bit of business done at Brown's house, located at Humboldt and Government Streets, a couple of minutes' stroll from today's Empress Hotel. The sentence put Brown in leg irons again for a three-month stretch on the chain gang.

One morning, two senior police officers, Sergeant George Blake and Superintendent Horace Smith, caught sight of Charlie sitting beside John Guest on Guest's delivery wagon. Recognizing Brown immediately, the suspicious officers decided to tail them. As they watched the wagon roll toward Rock Bay Bridge, the policemen concluded its destination was the new Songhees reserve on the north shore of the Inner Harbour.

The policemen raced down to the water's edge and either found or commandeered a boat and breathlessly rowed across the harbour. Gaining the beach, they cut through the brush and watched Brown manhandle a number of 10-gallon cans, obviously heavy with alcohol, off the wagon and into the hands of four Songhees. Hunkered down in the brush, Blake and Smith devised a plan. A minute or so after Brown and Guest rolled away from their customers, Superintendent Smith jumped aboard behind the two startled men, arrested them and ordered them to keep rolling—right up to the door of the jail.

Meanwhile, back on the reserve, Sergeant Blake was ducking rocks flung by the four screaming Songhees. Then one of the four rushed him. Blake didn't want to shoot anybody, but decided that the quicker he ended this, the likelier it was that he would survive. He swung his revolver down hard on the head of the grasping, gouging Native. He heard a grunt, felt his assailant relax his hold and watched the man slump to the ground. The rain of rocks stopped, and the panting, bruised policeman watched his attackers vanish. One prisoner wasn't as good as four, but it was a lot better than being stoned or beaten to death.

Justice Pemberton fined Brown $500 and Guest $100. After all, Guest hadn't actually sold anything; he had merely been hired to deliver the alcohol to Brown's customers. The men paid the fines. Guest stayed on the right side of the law after that. Brown couldn't, and just one week later he was arrested again for selling liquor. Out of cash, Brown was sentenced to wear leg irons for a year. During this incarceration, jailer Charles Wright was told to move the prisoner to another cell.

"You lay a hand on me you son of a bitch and I'll murder you," Brown warned Wright.

That didn't stop the jailer. As the two jostled and stumbled about the cell, Brown managed to get a headlock on Wright. The jailer's hands were still free, so he drew his revolver and pressed the muzzle to Brown's ear. "Let go or I'll blow your head off," Wright gasped. Brown simply tightened his hold. Wright squeezed the trigger. The resulting shot tore off Brown's ear, giving him both a nickname and an unusual appearance that later made it easy for lawmen to identify him. The new charge was assaulting a police officer and the sentence another year in the clink.

By now, it was obvious, perhaps even to One Ear, that for some reason the good fortune enjoyed by so many others in the liquor trade did not extend to him. So after feigning illness and being admitted to hospital, Brown escaped from the ward. "If he has left the island," a police spokesman snorted, "it's good riddance."

The former liquor seller had indeed left the island. He'd decided to try his hand at horse stealing and headed to the Kootenays, where a gold rush provided lots of opportunities. But Charlie still couldn't get it right. Near Wild Horse Creek, the horse rustler was arrested at gunpoint by a provincial policeman. When the rookie constable foolishly turned away, Brown whipped his hand beneath his coat, pulled his gun and shot the lawman in the back of the head. With that fatal move, Brown added murder to his roster of offences.

Learning of the shooting, four Wild Horse prospectors tracked the killer across the border and into Washington territory. When they realized they had actually overtaken Brown near Walla Walla, they lay in wait for him and provided a bloodthirsty climax to the story. The account titillated readers of New Westminster's *British Columbian*. The vigilantes "raised their . . . double-barrelled guns, loaded with buckshot, and fired simultaneously, literally riddling his dastardly carcass," the newspaper reported. "Returning the following day, they dug a hole into which they put the remains of Charles Brown," whisky seller, horse thief and, at the last, "cowardly murderer."

The violence that many terrified colonists had anticipated for years finally broke out in the spring of 1864. "Horrible Massacre!" the *Daily Chronicle* screamed. A band of Tsilhqot'in, including a chief who Waddington said had once called him his best friend, attacked Waddington's slumbering work crew just before dawn, shooting and stabbing nine men to death. The next day, at an advance camp up the Homathko River, they killed four more. Regaining the plateau, the Tsilhqot'in shot William Manning, the operator of a Puntzi Lake ranch and roadhouse. Manning's partner, Alex McDonald, leader of Waddington's second road crew, was leading his pack train south from Bella Coola. A few days after Manning's murder, McDonald, two of his men and the Tsilhqot'in "klootchman" of his second-in-command were shot and killed in an ambush. Stunned colonists had two questions. How had it happened? Why had it happened?

Initially, the sole incentive for the bloody attacks appeared to be plunder. After all, what else could motivate Natives to kill a crew that had treated them, as the *Colonist* put it, "in the kindest manner"? As expected, Waddington claimed that he and his crew were "guiltless" of any provocation. After Chartres Brew's on-site assessment of both the road's progress and conditions at the camps, colonists began to reconsider the earlier assumptions. While plunder was an obvious result of the attacks, the causes appeared to be revenge and fear. The Tsilhqot'in were angry about the catastrophic effects of smallpox and, more recently, the refusal by Waddington's men to pay for work with food, the starving Natives' priority. Brew's reports suggested that desperate women had been debased, forced to barter their bodies with the crew in order to feed their families.

The Tsilhqot'in's worst fear was disease. On two occasions, whites apparently used fear of smallpox as a weapon to control the unruly Natives. One of the crewmen (likely the foreman) in the Homathko Canyon and William Manning on the plateau were reported to have threatened the Tsilhqot'in with the dreaded pox. The Tsilhqot'in's terror turned to fury.

For decades, colonists had lived in growing dread of frenzied attacks by intoxicated Natives. How ironic then, that when all the presumed causes of what became known as the Chilcotin War were debated, liquor wasn't even mentioned as a potential contributing factor leading to the bloody mayhem. In that respect, at least, Waddington and his crew seemed truly "guiltless."

Not surprisingly, Frederick Seymour was anxious to cement peaceful relations with the colony's indigenous peoples. Brew was still investigating the killings at Bute Inlet and government representatives were still organizing the manhunt for the Tsilhqot'in when the mainland governor used the Queen's birthday celebration to demonstrate the benevolent might of British rule. Skilfully rehearsed by Roman Catholic missionaries, dozens of Fraser River chiefs paddled down to New Westminster to attend a sumptuous May 24 luncheon, say a few carefully chosen words to the white leader and hear what he had to say in return. "Please protect us from any bad Indians or any bad white men," three delegates asked Seymour. In case anyone wondered just what was meant by "bad white men," Seymour made it plain in his response. "I am glad to find that you have given up strong drinks," he told the assembled throng, "They are not good for you." Then he promised, "I shall protect you both from bad white men and from bad Indians."

Five years later, Seymour followed up personally on his pledge. In May 1869, in response to liquor-induced warfare near the Alaska border, he ventured north in the gunboat HMS *Sparrowhawk*. The conflict was not between Native and white, but between two north-coast tribes, the Tsimshian and the Nass. *Sparrowhawk* took into custody the whisky schooner *Nanaimo Packet*, whose trading cargo was alleged to have caused the hostilities. At Fort Simpson, Seymour added his signature and seal to a peace document signed by both warring parties. At a hearing held the next day into *Nanaimo Packet*'s alleged whisky trading, the schooner was confiscated and its captain fined $500.

Seymour never lived to complete his return voyage to New Westminster. In its story, the *Colonist* reported that "the cause of [Seymour's] death was dysentery." *Sparrowhawk*'s surgeon knew better, and before long—informally, of course—so did many residents of the unified island-mainland Colony of British Columbia. "Governor Seymour who had for some time been debilitated, called upon me for medical advice June 6th," Dr. Comrie wrote in his official journal, three days after *Sparrowhawk* had left Fort Simpson. "I found him suffering from great gastric irritation, nervous tremors, sleeplessness and other symptoms of alcoholism." The governor was too hungover even to stagger up on deck during a stop at Skidegate, where he had been expected to visit the workings of the Queen Charlotte Coal Company. Unsuccessful attempts were made to withhold liquor, "for which the patient had an inordinate craving which he gratified in spite of the vigilance of his servant and private secretary." According to the doctor, on Seymour's last night, "he succeeded in getting hold of a bottle of brandy and drinking it off."

Elderly John Tod, former HBC chief trader and colonial council member, bluntly related the truth to a friend in a letter, saying what newspapers could not. Seymour's death was due to "a long course of intemperance, which he had fatally indulged in." In short, the man who had reminded assembled chiefs that strong drinks "are not good for you," had lost his personal battle with the bottle and may have drunk himself to death.

By 1873, the BC Constabulary had become, with the colony's entry into Canada in 1871, the BC Provincial Constabulary. The name had changed, but the main problem that had vexed the late Chartres Brew, commissioner of police, still frustrated both the force and citizens who sought its protection. The constabulary was pitifully small. Twenty-two men were responsible for law enforcement throughout a quarter-million square miles of territory, addressing the complaints and concerns of about 10,000 non-Native residents. Miles from New Westminster, Victoria and Nanaimo—the three largest centres of population—residents of many small communities rarely saw a policeman. In addition to a growing number of duties, the men of the tiny force were responsible for somehow reining in what appeared to be increased Native drunkenness at a time when a BC Native could only get a drink from his own still or from a bootlegger's bottle.

Lean, bearded John Sullivan took the problem of Native liquor supply seriously, quite correctly considering it to be one of BC's major legal and social concerns. Sullivan held two jobs, superintendent of the provincial constabulary and Victoria's police chief. A lesser man might have bridled at the double duties, but Sullivan rose to the challenge. The twin roles provided a unique opportunity to strike at the illicit Native liquor trade on two fronts: in the city, where the distributors who supplied coastal liquor peddlers had their operations, and up the coast, where their couriers and sales teams—including Natives themselves—made the sales.

Sadly, Sullivan found it extremely difficult to arrest and successfully prosecute what were, to most appearances, well-respected city businessmen. Besides, he didn't have the men to search every vessel leaving Victoria's busy harbour in order to find crucial evidence. Having no other reasonable option, Sullivan decided to attack the sellers and their couriers up the coast. Arresting suspects was easy but getting courtroom convictions was not.

Police had to apprehend the suspect with alcohol in his possession and with third-party witnesses present. The witness-and-arrest game was much more difficult to play out on the open water than on land. Paddling around the Gulf of Georgia's channels and inlets, it was easy for whisky men to spot a naval vessel, its billowing smokestack visible miles from their canoes and small sailing boats. Traders simply dumped their liquid wares overboard and feigned innocence, smiling at fuming naval officers.

Both Sullivan and his superior, Attorney General George Walkem, realized that up-island officers were in a better geographical position to chase down traders; however, Walkem had good reasons for wanting Sullivan on the job. Years before, when Walkem was the MLA for Quesnel Forks District, Sullivan had fought to reapprehend an escaped Native murder suspect. Sullivan had no trouble remembering the incident; every time he removed his shirt, the scars from cuts and stab wounds inflicted by the suspect's knife were visible reminders of his life-and-death struggle.

Sullivan's "determination of character," as Walkem later put it, definitely made him Walkem's man. If decisive action was needed, the Attorney General was confident Sullivan wouldn't hesitate to do his duty. "Can I seize any liquor I find?" Sullivan asked his boss.

"Yes," Walkem said and then further suggested that the superintendent adopt the strategy of Victoria constables and empty out cans of liquor "wherever he found them."

Instead of using an expensive, easy-to-spot steam vessel, John Sullivan and his guide paddled up the coast in a large canoe. At Alert Bay, near the northern tip of the island, he investigated the murder of a Native by a storekeeper. James McGrath willingly confessed to killing Coma-Cow-Coma. McGrath had caught him stealing from his woodpile and bounced a rock off him. No one was more surprised than McGrath when the thief fell to the ground, dead. Liquor investigations would have to wait; Sullivan and his guide set off for Victoria with murder suspect McGrath and two witnesses.

Three days later, Sullivan spotted six canoes with liquor-to-trade flags fluttering from their masts. "I think I'll see if they have whisky," he decided. As the superintendent closed in, the alerted Native traders began to paddle away. "Nika tyhee policeman Victoria!" Sullivan yelled in Chinook trade talk. "Nika tikoo nannich mika whisky!" Paddles flashed; the Natives had no intention of stopping for any policeman looking for liquor. As the nearest canoe sped past, one of the bunch jumped up on a low box and screamed that the policeman and others like him were "dogs."

Drawing his revolver, Sullivan ordered his guide to

make for a second canoe. A warning shot whizzed across the bow as they cut the canoe off. "My gun went off by accident," Sullivan confessed in Chinook to the startled crew, "but I don't intend to shoot you." The apprehensive Natives allowed Sullivan to confiscate a can of booze easily enough and then volunteered that there was "hiyou whisky" (lots of whisky) in a third canoe.

Yelling at those in the third canoe that he was a police chief—his regulation peaked cap made it obvious—Sullivan watched a woman throw a blanket over some four-gallon cans. "I want that whisky!" he shouted. As the two canoes bumped together, Sullivan stood, leaned over and attempted to snatch up one of the cans.

"No!" the woman screamed and threw her body over the concealing blanket.

"Klosh Nannich—nika pooh mika!" (Look out or I'll shoot you) Sullivan warned.

One Native dropped his paddle. "Go ahead and shoot!" he yelled defiantly and then dove for a lidded wooden box. Boxes like the one he snatched up were familiar to James McGrath, and he knew what was usually inside them.

"Watch out!" Sullivan's murder suspect yelled. "He's got a gun!" The superintendent moved quickly. Slipping his own cocked revolver from right hand to left, he leaned over and grabbed for the wooden container. The canoes rocked as the two men jerked back and forth. The Native reached for Sullivan's revolver. Sullivan fought him off with one hand and tugged at the box with the other. Sullivan's opponent managed to yank the box away, then wrapped his hand around the revolver resting inside. The superintendent levelled his own weapon.

Crack! The Native jerked backwards, his neck spurting blood, as his weapon slipped from his hand and thumped to the bottom of the canoe. The wounded man stooped to retrieve it.

Crack! The Native collapsed out of sight.

"Behind you!" McGrath yelled. Sullivan whirled. In the stern of the canoe, another man was slipping a musket from beneath a blanket, its muzzle pointed at the superintendent's chest. In a confused combination of Chinook and English, Sullivan shouted to the man to "Mash [drop] that musket!" Staring unblinkingly at the policeman, the rifleman continued to uncover the long gun.

Crack! The murderous trader slumped over his partly concealed weapon.

At the sound of Sullivan's gunfire, muskets erupted from other canoes. A few minutes before, their crews had been anxious to flee. Now, eager to avenge their gunshot tribesmen, they closed in on the policeman. There was no way Sullivan and his small party could fight them all and survive. It was time to make a run for it. "Push off!" he ordered his guide. Bullets splattered the water all about them, but the superintendent and his party managed to escape.

Once in Victoria, Sullivan duly reported the incident to

George Walkem, who immediately recognized a problem. Selling whisky to Natives was merely a misdemeanour; one didn't shoot a man down—Native or white—on suspicion of a misdemeanour. Still, the traders had been shot while resisting arrest, so Sullivan had acted out of self-defence. However, the Attorney General cautioned his superintendent that he might eventually have to go to trial over the matter. For the moment, the two men decided to let sleeping dogs lie.

Within days, this particular dog was kicked into wakefulness by David Higgins, editor of the *Daily British Colonist*. A virulent combination of fear, the public perception of refined society and the general distaste with what the *Daily British Colonist* called "the present imbecile [provincial] administration," conspired to cast Superintendent Sullivan in the role of villain.

The *Colonist* had warned Sullivan not to go up the coast alone, Higgins reminded his readers. The editor, however, didn't really care about Sullivan's well-being; he was worried about everybody else's. By travelling alone, Sullivan had simply invited problems—Native problems—that the government should have been attempting to avoid. As government employee, the superintendent had earlier proved himself nothing but a "Champion Whitewasher," who claimed that the Natives, at least in the Comox area, were "so affectionate and peaceable that a policeman was unnecessary the length and breadth of the coast." Now, Higgins gloated, "We are glad that he is the first to realize the utter folly and stupidity of his report and the unhappy results of the government policy which he was sent up expressly to 'whitewash' at provincial expense."

Despite the lesson of the Chilcotin War, Higgins's umbrage masked the old fear of liquor-stoked Natives on the warpath. Like many others, Higgins expected Natives to avenge what he called an "East Coast Homicide" on any white person they happened across, including "exposed settlers and solitary way-farers." Now, the editor sputtered, "we have two Indians killed and perhaps an Indian War inaugurated."

Warring Natives might prove deadly, especially to up-island settlements such as Comox and even a town the size of Nanaimo. (Thank heavens it had not destroyed its for-tified bastion!) Perhaps more important, the mere idea of white-Native warfare was totally repugnant to the citizens of respectable Victoria. Many British Columbians feared an "Indian War" might, in the minds of Dominion politicians in Ottawa as well as relatives back in England, link BC with the contemptible (or, at least, lamentable) American Wild West, in which the blazing six-guns of Wild Bill Hickok and his ilk were lauded, and where Indian massacres occurred with disturbing regularity. The raucous Cariboo Gold Rush was now a slightly embarrassing memory; the province didn't need bloody frontier incidents to tarnish its image as a very civilized part of Canada's vast Dominion and, indeed, of the British Empire itself.

Quick-shooting John Sullivan, who clearly represented

the best-forgotten past, became a convenient embodiment of everything that was wrong with the present "imbecile" government. The *Colonist* pilloried the superintendent, proceeding to "utterly and wholly condemn him for the reckless and foolhardy manner in which he provoked a conflict with a superior force."

Sensitive to the uproar, the government initiated an investigation. A man of honour and conscience, Sullivan ordered a constable to charge him with murder. As the legal examination process crawled through late May, the government undertook some damage control. Justice Pemberton was heading up the coast on HMS *Boxer* to locate witnesses for the Sullivan trial, and perhaps suspects as well. Israel Wood Powell, superintendent of Indian Affairs, packed his bags and climbed *Boxer*'s gangway, eager to wave the flag and shake hands with coastal chiefs. Happily for Sullivan and the provincial government, before the superintendent could face the Court of Assize's grand jury, Powell was back and beaming. The Natives, it seemed, were a long, long way from the warpath. Everywhere Powell went, the *Colonist* reported, "he was received with open arms by the natives and welcomed as their Great Chief."

Before a throng of courtroom spectators—the *Colonist* had helped make the case a *cause célèbre*—Sullivan, charged with both wilful murder and shooting with intent (one of the wounded men still lived) pleaded not guilty. James McGrath, murder suspect and witness for the defence, took the stand.

Evidence was presented. Finally, on June 21, the jury received its instructions and left to consider its verdict and the super-intendent's fate. The jury was back in the courtroom just 15 minutes later. It found there was not enough evidence to bring the case to a petty jury, the next step in legal proceed-ings. Sullivan's fate would be decided here and now.

Foreman J.W. Cary told the judge and assembled multitude that the jury found the superintendent guilty—if that was the word—of justifiable homicide. The jury, Cary quickly added, "wished to take this opportunity of congratulating the government on having an officer who so efficiently and energetically discharged his duty." Applauded and cheered by friends and colleagues, the *Colonist* reported, the discharged superintendent "left the Court without a stain on his character." David Higgins, however, had the last word on the matter. Sullivan's type of "efficiency and energy," the *Colonist* editor sniffed, was something "the country desires to see no more."

It didn't see much more of it from Sullivan. The man who had triumphed over knives and guns was soon defeated by those who wielded pens: bottom-line bureaucrats. More and more duties were heaped upon his shoulders and those of his men, while civil servants stroked out items in the force's diminishing budget. A man of principle—and perhaps self-preservation—John Sullivan resigned from government service just two years after he walked out of Victoria's courthouse.

5

Saloon Culture

IT'S A PIVOTAL SCENE IN hundreds of motion picture and television westerns. Against the tinkle of a tuneless piano, we hear the clink of spurs and the thud of boot heels on the boardwalk outside. Someone is approaching the spring-mounted doors of the saloon. A grizzled, narrow-eyed man—the good guy or the bad guy?—appears in the doorway, pauses briefly to survey the noisy, smoky scene inside and then pushes through the doors. The stranger saunters up to the bar. "Whisky," he tells the white-aproned bartender.

This archetypical scene is based on the reality of the western frontier saloon. Much has been made of the fact that the West was populated almost entirely by men. In the coastal

British colonies of 1865, the male to female ratio amongst immigrants was 100 to 1. Men lived without the moderating influences of women, enduring a frontier life devoid of leisure or cultural pursuits. This, pundits say, explains the drinking. It was the only recreation in this masculine society and, on the West Coast, the only release from physical toil for hard-working loggers, fishermen and miners.

This explanation sounds logical, except that by the time the American Civil War reached its bloody conclusion in 1865, and with the Wild West yet to come, saloon culture was already established in the civilized East. For years, millions of men had been walking up to bars—inside crude shanties on slum alleyways or plush, stylish facilities on fashionable avenues—and uttering the word "whisky." They did it in spite of the influence of wives and children. They did it in spite of Sunday sermons. They did it in spite of the many intellectual, artistic and sporting opportunities available in cities such as Philadelphia, New York, Baltimore and even staid Toronto. When Americans, Canadians and Old World immigrants moved westward, it was only logical that they carried with them a prodigious thirst for booze.

In new, green-lumber towns, the saloon sign was up before almost any other, often hammered onto the rough-cut supports of a tent. More permanent watering holes were usually built before almost any other establishments. By the summer of 1859, the little Fraser River hamlet of Yale was a drunkard's paradise. Visiting Wesleyan

Methodist missionaries viewed it as the gateway to Hades. The Lord's Day, for miners on the river's bars, was also shopping and drinking day, during which, as Dr. Ephraim Evans told the readers of Toronto's *Christian Guardian*, "There is a fearful amount of Sabbath desecration."

In 1866, the overnight construction of the newest colonial gold town in the Columbia River's Big Bend territory clearly demonstrated miners' priorities. Seymour City boasted 13 stores, 2 blacksmith shops, a livery stable and, not so incidentally, 2 breweries and 6 saloons to slake the thirst of its few hundred gold-seeking residents. A few years earlier, as BC's gold seekers ventured through the Fraser Canyon and tramped over the 400-mile route that became the Cariboo Road, it was the same story over and over again from Yale to Camerontown.

Based on descriptions at the time, at least two of the rough-hewn frontier Cariboo saloons rivalled those on more civilized avenues of Victoria and New Westminster. The penultimate bar in Barkerville was Barry and Adler's Fashion Saloon, advertised as "the largest and most complete saloon in British Columbia," featuring "Card Room, Bar Room and Billiard Saloon." In neighbouring Camerontown, proprietor James Loring's Terpsychorean Saloon (from the Greek Terpsichore, meaning "delight in dancing") introduced an attraction that would become the stuff of legend: German dance-hall women called hurdy-gurdy girls.

Miners lined up inside the Terpsychorean for a chance to whirl a gurdy over the wooden dance floor to tunes pounded out on Williams Creek's only piano, shipped especially for Loring from Victoria. Then, gurdies and prospectors would proceed to a bar "stocked with the finest Liquors and Segars" for as many drinks as the feminine gold diggers could pry out of prospectors' pokes. Each sober, fruit juice–imbibing gurdy kept half the sum—after Loring had taken his commission. The girls were the inspiration for a Cariboo poet, Scotsman James Anderson, to offer up six stanzas in the style of Robbie Burns, including the lines:

> They danced at nicht in dresses light,
> Frae late until the early, O!
> But oh! Their hearts were hard as flint,
> Which vexed the laddies sairly, O!
> The dollar was their only love,
> And that they lo'ed fu' dearly, O!
> The daftest hour that ere I spent,
> Was dancin' wi' the hurdies, O!

For Terpsychorean patrons, it was dancing and drinks—but nothing else. The gurdies weren't prostitutes, as many saloon dancers and entertainers were in Seattle, Washington, and later in Dawson City, Yukon. That "degraded set," according to Barkerville's weekly *Cariboo Sentinel*, favoured "male attire and swagger through the saloons and miners camps with cigars or huge quids of tobacco in their mouths, cursing and swearing and look anything but the angels in petticoats heaven intended they should be."

Meanwhile, accompanied by his Native wife and other members of her family, stout, bearded New Westminster saloon owner John "Gassy Jack" Deighton paddled a dugout canoe around today's Point Grey and up Burrard Inlet. Deighton looked over at "Sue" Moody's mill on the north shore and at Captain Edward Stamp's sawmill and thought about all the men working the captain's 30,000 leased acres of timber. There wasn't much for mill workers do in the 1867 rainforest, unless they wanted to row three miles up the inlet to North Road, then make the long nine-mile walk through the rainforest over the Royal Engineers' Trail (the route of which approximates today's Kingsway thoroughfare) to emerge, finally, at New Westminster. Deighton knew only one objective would goad a man to undertake this trek and endure the agony of the long stumble back the next day. At New Westminster, he could drink 'til he dropped. There was nowhere to do that on the inlet.

Deighton, whose garrulousness earned him the "Gassy" sobriquet, recognized the opportunity and seized it. He approached mill hands and told them if they helped him build a saloon on the south side of the inlet, they wouldn't have to walk too far to get a drink. The Globe Saloon was up within 24 hours. Other buildings were soon erected around the new watering hole, and the tiny settlement was named Gastown, after the man who started it all. Later, it was renamed Granville, and finally, in 1884, Vancouver.

Nothing Gassy Jack's mill-worker construction crew could erect in a day could resemble the gambling and drinking palaces of that west coast metropolis, San Francisco, or even most establishments in little Victoria. The Deighton's Globe was little more than a shack, not unlike other drinking establishments up and down the coast and further inland as well, where customer service could be as crude as the facility.

Inside a primitive Kootenay gold-camp saloon, a visiting Englishman surveyed the few bottles standing on the board shelves behind the rough wood counter. "I will have a dry martini," he blithely informed the bartender.

"Like Hell you will," the barkeep growled. "You'll have straight Scotch out of a tin cup like everybody else."

By the 1870s, the culture of the saloon was deeply entrenched in society from coast to coast and would remain so for decades. Throughout most of the 19th century, there were repeated efforts to prohibit the Natives' use of liquor. The percentage of heavy drinkers in any town and city likely far exceeded that of heavy drinkers on most Native reserves, yet there was almost no mid-19th century agitation to prohibit non-Native drinking, except that of southern slaves.

Statistics leave no doubt as to the significant role saloons played in everyday West Coast pioneer life. To get a sense of this, it helps to compare 2012 reality with that of yesteryear. Today, the population of Hope, BC, is about 6,500. There are probably a couple of dozen places near the site of the old HBC Fort Hope where residents and visitors can walk in, sit down and order a drink or buy liquor to enjoy at home. In 1864 Victoria, with a population similar to Hope's present one, there were at least 149 establishments where thirsty customers could purchase a bottle or empty one. By 1870, Victoria's booze business was king; the city's four breweries and two distilleries outnumbered any other specific type of manufacturing operation—lumber, soapworks, foundry, tanneries or shipyards.

Potential saloon patrons usually didn't have to go far to slake their thirst. By the 1880s, Nanaimo's community of 6,000 contained 21 legal watering holes, and perhaps dozens of others operated without paying government licence fees. By 1880, a licensed bar existed for every 13 residents in the province's largest mainland city, New Westminster. It was the same, of course, south of the 49th parallel. By the 1890s, Everett, a Puget Sound city of less than 30,000 souls, boasted 40 saloons, and by 1909, even tiny south Washington's Pasco—population 2,000—was home to 66 drinking establishments. In the two-year period between 1889 and 1890, Washington State beer sales increased by 33 percent.

An image of a bygone era—the turn-of-the-century saloon. This Everett, Washington, bar boasts a large wall-mounted mirror, hidden behind a covering to avoid the reflected glare from the photographer's exploding flash powder. On the floor are round cuspidors, designed to catch customers' expectorated tobacco juice. UNIVERSITY OF WASHINGTON LIBRARIES, SPECIAL COLLECTIONS UW32329

In the second half of the 19th century, it was common for men in the Pacific Northwest to drink repeatedly, morning, noon and night, on an almost daily basis. Most drinking was done in saloons (drinking in the privacy of one's home only came into vogue when 20th-century prohibition laws closed up every other alternative). Many saloons established no age limit; young teenagers dropped in for a quick one after work in the forests or fields, or on the way home from school. One other potential source of liquor was the friendly merchant. Men may have come in to purchase a bag of potatoes or a new shirt, but retailers knew what their customers really wanted. Many merchants filled pails with whisky, surrounding them with cups so that patrons could refresh themselves for free.

Even in the midst of rampant saloon culture, the laws of commerce applied. Theoretically, the liquor market had a saturation point (to use a particularly fitting turn of phrase), where supply exceeded demand. By 1910, Spokane saloon keepers must have wondered if they had reached that point. One hundred and twenty-three saloons vied for business in the city of about 50,000, even though boom times were over, and so-called "job sharks" were taking money from the unemployed to help them find jobs. Saloon owner James "Jimmie" Durkin, an Irish armchair philosopher with a twinkle in his eye, was out to beat the competition.

Durkin was a non-stop promotion machine with a lot to promote: three saloons, one of which was an imposing two-storey, stone-faced building on a major downtown corner. Not content to merely serve drinks at his bars and tables, Jimmie urged customers to take some home with them in economy-sized one- and two-gallon jugs, all emblazoned with "Durkins Whiskies and Wines," "Durkins Three Stores" and "Durkins Whiskies and Liquors," and he sold wholesale as well. Whisky came in eye-catching, triangular, red glass containers nicknamed "megaphone" bottles. The Durkins name was everywhere, even painted on a series of large boulders lining the main route into the city. By the time they reached downtown, parched stagecoach passengers knew exactly where to go.

Some fascinating statistics on liquor consumption were published in the aftermath of the 1890s Canadian Royal Commission on the Liquor Traffic. Calculating consumption for the year 1893, the commission reported that the average Canadian consumed .597 gallons of liquor. Quebec imbibers knocked back .672 gallons, more than in any province or territory east of the Rockies. However, the average BC tippler gulped down 1.26 gallons, more per capita than residents of any other Canadian province or territory. To supply the growing number of free-standing saloons and hotel bars, BC brewers went on a building binge. In 1880, there were just nine legitimate breweries operating in the entire province. A decade later—just three years after the first passenger train huffed into Vancouver—that small number had doubled. By 1900, 41 breweries supplied suds to BC's beer drinkers.

Across the border, brewing was even bigger business, and competition was intense. In the biggest of many amalgamations, four companies with operations in Portland, Seattle and Walla Walla disappeared and a new corporate name was nailed on the walls—Portland and Seattle Breweries, head office, London, England. News of the "wet" coast profits had travelled far indeed.

Many breweries remained small, their crews rolling

kegs onto large wagons for delivery to local bars. A brewer's distribution area was limited to a six-horse team's work day. Moreover, the product itself did not lend itself to market expansion. Beer was unpasteurized and had a short shelf life, and refrigeration was rare. By the 1890s, however, technology had made beer barons' expansions feasible; innovative bottle-fed machines installed the newly patented "crown" cap, which made the bottles air-tight. Any brewery located alongside a railway siding—another innovation— could fill boxcars with bottled beer and ship its product to saloons and bars hundreds of miles away.

Like other entrepreneurs, brewers realized that the coast's burgeoning and mostly male population represented a business bonanza. The industry first tapped the potential, so to speak, by supplying beer, then by financing would-be saloon keepers, underwriting everything from liquor licences to bar fixtures. The number of saloons rose exponentially up and down the coast.

The new business operators' first flush of pride and prestige was soon replaced by heart-racing anxiety, as the pressure to increase sales mounted in a business environment made fiercely competitive by the very men who had financed them. The system turned many operators, most with limited management abilities, into little more than wage slaves. Saloons on both sides of the border were open for business seven days a week, with shifts of bartenders working around the clock. Increasingly, those in charge turned a blind eye to their community's social mores and laws and, finally, even to violence.

The result of all this was public drunkenness on a scale that is unimaginable today. As Canadian Pacific and Northern Pacific rails approached the coast in the 1880s, the situation went from bad to worse. Conditions in Yale were typical. The prospectors were gone, but now gangs of railroad-building navvies enriched Yale's drinking holes. "Drunkenness and disorder filled the place day and night," Protestant churchman Herbert Gowen reported. "Tattered, dirt-bespattered drunkards rolled about the streets, wallowing in the mud, cursing and fighting and driving all respectable people into the recesses of their homes, while saloon after saloon was added to the number already terribly in excess of the needs of the community."

The single saloon in Kiona, Washington, became the nightly destination of over 400 railroad workers. If they ventured near to the raucous site, wide-eyed residents could watch the barkeeps literally throwing the semi-comatose drunks out the back door where they landed, retching and shaking, in a tangle of arms and legs. As late as 1914, Seattle's *Argus* reported, "There are saloons in which fights are of nightly occurrence . . . where drunks are 'rolled' . . . where the man who gets his check cashed stands mighty little show of getting away with any of the coin . . . where liquor is sold to boys."

One of the reasons for the saloon's ascendancy was the

many guises the establishment assumed: bank, post office, café, casino, wedding chapel, and dance, meeting or music hall. On one occasion in early 1859, a bar near Fort Langley became a "field of honour," standing in for the usual quiet but potentially deadly space in some wooded area where two aggrieved parties paced off their destinies, turned and aimed pistols at one another. Fuelled by the contents of the bar's bottles, two quarrelsome and none-too-sober gents prepared to do the deadly deed a few feet from the bartender. Matthias Neil appears to have been too befuddled to get off the first shot. However, by accident or design, his hapless opponent blasted a hole in the floorboards, either because he nervously squeezed the trigger before he meant to, or because he hoped Neil would follow suit and they would both belly up to the bar to toast their futures, once confident they both had one. Neil took no further chances. He raised his revolver, got off three quick shots and sent his fellow duellist to meet his maker.

Inside Fort Langley's courtroom-of-the-moment, Judge Matthew Begbie listened carefully to witnesses and considered the evidence. Then, given the curious set of circumstances in which he found himself, he very consciously gave extremely impartial instructions to the jury. It happened that the accused sitting anxiously in the prisoner's box was no stranger to the judge. Incarcerated at Fort Victoria, Neil had made the trip up the Fraser for trial on the same paddlewheeler as Begbie, who was on his initial circuit of the area. Two nights before, in the company of Arthur Bushby and others, judge and prisoner had shared an on-board dinner in a most companionable manner.

The jury left to consider its verdict. Hours later—urged on by the judge in a written note and then by a personal visit to what passed for a jury room—the reticent jurymen finally delivered one. "Manslaughter," the foreman announced. Two days later, in New Westminster, Neil appeared before the judge and was sentenced to four years behind bars.

For Judge Begbie, the sentencing presented a teachable moment. To the crowd of American prospectors who gathered for the sentencing of one of their own by a bewigged Britisher addressed absurdly as "My Lord," it was a very important lesson. In the British colony where they dug for gold, taking a life had dire consequences. The judge backed up his words with an American law book. The *Victoria Gazette* saw the news value in the story. Shortly afterward, so did at least one San Francisco journal.

Quoting the *Gazette*, the startled *Daily Bulletin* went on to say that in California, "The circumstances of one party attacking, or firing first, is usually considered as sufficient excuse for the other party following up and killing his antagonist." How much different was the situation in Her Majesty's colonies of Vancouver Island and British Columbia! The timing of this surprising news was propitious. Hundreds of potential American prospectors were ready to set sail for the Fraser and thousands more would follow. The Begbie news item may have been one of the reasons why colonial lawlessness remained the exception rather than the rule. Nevertheless, as whisky-war sagas attest, and in spite of future opinions to the contrary, the British colonies definitely qualified as part of the Wild West.

Inside a Williams Lake saloon—perhaps the roadhouse built and operated by police constable William Pinchbeck (a bottle of whisky was four dollars and drinks 25 cents a shot)—an American named Gilchrist attempted to shoot and kill a man named Turner. Gilchrist was a loser in more ways the one, but the losing that sparked the gunplay came about at the faro table where Turner beat him twice in a row. As Turner rose to walk to the bar with his winnings, he couldn't resist smiling down at the losing punter and asking, "Is there any game you can play better than this one?"

Yes, there was, Gilchrist figured: the deadly game of shoot to kill. There at the table, the sore loser hatched a plot with some buddies. As planned, Gilchrist and a friend began to "quarrel" loudly. Then they drew their shootin' irons. Playing their parts, Gilchrist's friends leaped to their feet and attempted to wrestle away his gun. What Gilchrist was supposed to do was swing about so he could "accidentally" shoot Turner, now standing at the bar. Except when Gilchrist pulled the trigger, the bullet intended for Turner buried itself in a saloon habitué snoozing on the bar a foot or two away, killing him instantly. What happened later inside Williams Lake's new courthouse was as bizarre as the crime itself.

Matthew Baillie Begbie, the Colony of British Columbia's first judge, as he appeared at the height of the Cariboo gold rush. Begbie presided over circuit court in small gold towns throughout BC. UNIVERSITY OF BRITISH COLUMBIA, RARE BOOKS AND SPECIAL COLLECTIONS EX-4-35

When Gilchrist was brought before Begbie, he was tried by, quite literally, a jury of his peers—Americans all and not a few of them fugitives from justice in Washington and Oregon Territories. After the incontrovertible evidence of Gilchrist's guilt had been presented, Begbie condemned the practice of carrying firearms and warned the jury against allowing sympathy or the accidental nature of the killing to cloud their visions. Their clear-cut duty was to find Gilchrist guilty of murder. That verdict, jury members knew, was a gallows offence.

Thirty minutes later, the jury returned a verdict of manslaughter. Gilchrist's shoulders slumped in relief; he had cheated the hangman! Seething, the judge turned to the prisoner and sentenced him "only to imprisonment for life. I feel I am, through some incomprehensible reason, prevented from doing my proper duty. Your crime was unmitigated, diabolical murder. You deserved to be hanged!" Begbie fumed, perhaps unwittingly inspiring his undeserved reputation as the "Hanging Judge." "Had the jury performed their duty I might now have the painful satisfaction of condemning you to death." The judge twisted about, "And you, gentlemen of the jury!" he bellowed. "You are a pack of Dalles [Oregon] horse thieves, and permit me to say, it would give me great pleasure to see *you* hanged, each and every one of you, for declaring a murderer guilty only of manslaughter!"

It's not surprising that so much violence occurred in or around saloons. Men—becoming more inebriated by the hour—spent more time in them than in their dim, dismal lodgings. In 1909, when one frightened saloon keeper in the murderous little Washington mill town of Aberdeen (nicknamed the Port of Missing Men) called it quits, he confessed to the Spokane *Spokesman-Review* that he made his decision after a total of 69 residents were killed by local bartenders and their molls within a single year.

By the late 1870s, Judge Begbie was no longer on the bench in frontier cabins, stores or saloons. He tried cases in courthouses. However, the judge might just as well have been holding court under tent-town canvas. Frontier feelings regarding acceptable saloon conduct hadn't changed, whether drinkers found themselves inside a brick-fronted downtown Victoria saloon or a clapboard frontier bar. In 1883, Irishman Davie Lavin had a punch-up with Johnston Robertson in Victoria's Regent Saloon. When Robertson went down at Lavin's hands, he stayed down and never regained his feet. Three days after Lavin laid Robertson low, an attending physician at Victoria's hospital pronounced him dead. Lavin was charged with murder.

Lavin's best defence may have been self-defence. The court heard evidence that Robertson had been involved in a series of fisticuffs earlier that afternoon. The man clearly had sealed his own fate by having one fight too many with the wrong man. Now the jury was charged with sealing the fate of the victor. As the jury deliberated, what likely remained unspoken (why state the obvious?) was the accepted notion that a man had a duty to defend himself—backing down was not an option. The jurymen, who were likely all drinkers, knew how a barroom brawl could quickly elevate to a contest perceived as something much nobler than the clumsy swing-and-miss dance it actually resembled. When surrounded by a crowd of men, the contest became a point of honour, even—and perhaps especially—if your assailant got the best of you and knocked you into oblivion. The loser could still walk into that saloon the next day holding his throbbing head high, and the odds were good his former opponent would stand him to a drink.

Begbie heard the details and scribbled in his bench book, "No evidence of sandbag [a club or cudgel] or other weapon." (By this time, the noun "sandbag" had also become a street-slang verb, and men sneered antagonistically of "sandbagging" their enemies.) Begbie gave the jurors their instructions, and they filed out to reach a verdict. When they filed back in, they acquitted the accused. Begbie was apoplectic. "Gentlemen of the jury, I have heard your verdict. Mind you, it's *your* verdict, not mine," he boomed. Begbie was only getting started. The significance of the jury's leniency, which was, at the very least, "at variance with the evidence," went far beyond the release of a saloon brawler.

"Many repetitions of conduct as yours will make trial by jury a horrible farce and the city of Victoria, which you inhabit, a nest of immorality and crime encouraged by immunity from the law which criminals will receive from the announcement of such verdicts as yours. I have nothing more to say to you." But Begbie still wasn't done. Turning on the delighted Davie Lavin, he thundered, "Prisoner, you are discharged! Go, and sandbag some of the jurymen! They deserve it!"

6

The Saloon Must Go!

THE STUNNED HUNTER STOPPED SHORT: a few yards away, a mother bear and her cubs ambled past. If she were to be wounded herself or watch one of her cubs take a musket ball, the she-bear would charge. A slowly loaded 1830s musket would never provide that lifesaving second shot. The hunter held his fire. He hesitated for another reason. There, even closer to the bears, two black-clad men knelt beneath one of the large elm trees that were abundant in Ohio's forests. They appeared to be praying—as well they might! Thankfully, the bears left the men untouched. At least, that's the legend.

What Presbyterian clergymen John Shipherd and Philo Stewart were praying for wasn't deliverance from bears (eyes closed, they remained ignorant of the animals' presence) but rather, heavenly guidance. When the awestruck hunter related his tale, the two knew they had chosen the right spot for their new community. Thus, Oberlin, Ohio, was founded not by hard-drinking prospectors or profanity-shouting sodbusters, but by two men of God disenchanted with western migrants' lack of Christian morals. The town's future prosperity would be based almost purely on righteousness.

Two decades after Shipherd and Stewart knelt in the forest, progressive Oberlin became a haven for southern slaves as the terminus of what was called the Underground Railroad, on which all "tracks" led north to freedom. Ohio backed up its charitable welcome to these frightened, desperate people with a writ of habeas corpus, protecting them from extradition back to their plantation masters.

So, in the 1890s, it was not by chance that a small group of Oberlin residents would champion what they considered the nation's most crucial cause: prohibition. The struggle would be long and hard, but they never doubted that they would succeed. After all, destiny was on their side. They called their new society the Anti-Saloon League (ASL); however, it wasn't America's first prohibition organization.

In late 1873, the Women's Christian Temperance Union (WCTU) was founded to create "a sober and pure world." The following year, as marching women prayed for temperance in Portland, Oregon, the WCTU formed a chapter in Washington Territory, where women conducted a "saloon siege" in Olympia, although, as the cynical Olympia *Standard* noted, when "the singing and praying ceases the drinking and dissipation commences."

The Anti-Saloon League was born out of desperation. As the league saw it, "please don't drink, please don't distill liquor" prohibition strategies were missing the mark. The league's chosen target was not the drinker or liquor manufacturer, but rather the places where manufacturers' products were sold and consumed. Thus, the ASL set itself a much easier objective to reach than that set by the high-minded WCTU. Instead of virtuously (and vainly) attempting to change individuals' drinking habits, the ASL chose a tangible target that people could see on every town's main street, and one that had already earned public enmity. It was easy to perceive the league not as a chastising scold but rather as the benevolent saviour of besotted husbands and fathers who were, after all, the pitiful victims of the vile saloon.

In Puget Sound communities, the post–Civil War temperance movement found its initial support not only from women, as is often supposed, but through the membership of the International Order of Good Templars, which advocated companionship, ritual and "clean manhood." Good Templar lodges were, in effect, non-alcoholic saloons, where abstaining members took shots, not from glasses, but around the facilities' pool tables, or instead of standing at a bar, sat comfortably in upholstered reading-room chairs.

By the 1880s, Templars, the WCTU and militant churches

had banded together to form a Territorial Temperance Alliance. The alliance claimed some early success when legislation forced saloons to close on Sundays and saloon keepers were made liable for injuries attributed to intoxication. In an era when the telegraph represented the only electronic communication, newspapers were the sole source of public information. By the 1880s, Seattle prohibitionists had become publishers. The Order of Good Templars' *Mirror* proclaimed an imminent "Temperance War" against what it called "saloonacy." Most people scoffed.

While temperance groups usually represented society's fringe element, interest in the ASL began to grow. By the early 20th century, the WCTU had become a scattergun whose members took aim at a host of "social gospel" targets, including Sunday golf and the sale of cigarettes to China. By contrast, the Anti-Saloon League—the name said it all—had just one clear objective: the obliteration of the saloon. An Anti-Saloon League yearbook later rationalized the league's objective very clearly. Liquor traffic, it stated, "beggars the individual, burdens the State and impoverishes the nation. It commercializes vice and capitalizes on human weakness. It impairs the public health; breaks the public peace, and debauches the public morals." Just two years after its inauguration, the ASL was so successful that Oberlin organizers founded a national body, the Anti-Saloon League of America. Three years later, in 1898, the national organization announced the formation of a Washington State affiliate.

The ASL's eventual Pacific Northwest success was rooted in its non-partisan appeal; it elevated itself above petty politics. Over time, Republicans, Democrats and members of the fledgling Prohibition Party became supporters. Moreover, it was easy to support: while ASL was anti-saloon, it most definitely was not anti-drink. Here, at last, was an organization around which moderates—and moderate drinkers—could rally. As a route to saloon closures, the ASL looked to the state's 30-year-old constitution, which included local option bills that allowed towns and cities, by majority vote, to prohibit "the sale or disposal of spirituous liquors." In Oregon, local option had become an initiative by 1904.

Turn-of-the-century "prohibs" in Washington and Oregon were convinced that alcoholic beverages were evil incarnate and the root cause of not only public drunkenness but a host of other social ills, including prostitution, gambling, venereal disease and poverty. In Spokane, Reverend E.H. Braden, a leading Baptist, remarked that Jimmie Durkin's saloon windows advertised booze, but not the terrible effects of imbibing it. Durkin decided to capitalize on the disparaging remarks. Spokane's liquor tycoon invited the Baptist minister to put prohibitionists' messages where it would do them the most good: in the windows of his two-storey saloon. Jimmie assured Braden there was no catch: "You can use all of my windows for any liquor displays you want. You can use anything you want, advertise anything you want, and I will not interfere. Also I will pay for everything. You can depend on me: I'm a man of my word."

Occupying eight windows, the resulting tableaux graphically illustrated the domestic evils of drink through large, colourful images of hard-drinking men and ravaged, ragged wives and children, flanked by gruesome statistics. The displays became the talk of the town. Durkin then placed ads in the *Spokesman-Review* inviting visiting Baptists (and, of course, anyone else) "to Inspect the Only Liquor Store in America Whose Windows Were Decorated by a Baptist Minister."

"A gigantic publicity stunt," the newspaper grumbled. Exactly, Durkin would have agreed. Just before Jimmie passed away, he had instructions for the inscription on his tombstone:

Jimmie Durkin
Born 1859 Died 1934
The minister said, "A man of his word."

As the 20th century neared, liquor's power created a particularly insidious trend: political influence. "For years and years, [the town of] Wilbur has been absolutely in the grasp of the liquor element," Marion Hay, Wilbur businessman and future Washington governor, admitted to a friend. "We only maintained control so long as we allowed the liquor interests to have a certain amount of freedom. In 1898 or '99, we raised the saloon license . . . to $1,000. At the next election they put us completely out," Hay recalled, "and from that time on they held absolute sway in Wilbur." In a strident sector fraught with infighting, the support of moderate Governor Hay gave the ASL respectability. "If a man wishes to buy liquor and take it home with him, that is his right," Hay wrote, "but what we [ASL supporters] wish to prevent is the open sale of liquor and the maintenance of the saloon."

As many Pacific Northwest organizations fighting the evils of liquor vied for attention and support, an individual captured the public's imagination. Arriving in Seattle just before the election of 1888, Edward B. Sutton was to remain a figurehead of the West Coast temperance movement for 20 years. Delivering a thousand speeches annually, Sutton lectured mainly to rural folks about what he called the Four Cornerstones of Christian Civilization: good morals, good education, good business principles and the spirit of love. In agrarian towns, Sutton was preaching mostly to the converted. For many in farm hamlets, saloons were the most visible sign of big-city vice and corruption, and, not so incidentally, what was politely referred to as the "foreign element." Immigrants stepping off trains were bringing their taste for vodka, wine and beer to coastal towns and cities.

Sutton understood the link between liquor and lawmakers. There was no chance of progressing to "the highest climax of Christian civilization," he maintained, as long as the liquor "oligarchy" existed and had "a hand in shaping legislation." Sutton was more than a mere prohibitionist; he had been an organizer of the 20-year-old Prohibition Party of the United States. As the territory prepared for statehood, Sutton took advantage of the approaching constitutional convention to propose a Washington State Temperance Alliance (WSTA), which, he explained, would work against the "deadly influence of the liquor traffic" and seek to "annihilate the drunkard-making business." Such an alliance would not support either Republican or Democratic candidates, but instead offer its own.

Constitutional ballots did more than ask the electorate if it was for or against the proposed state constitution and where the new capital should be located. Reflecting the era's reform movement, the ballot also asked whether they supported women's suffrage and—thanks to WSTA petitioning—whether voters supported prohibition.

The weekly *Leader*—a joint publication of the Templars, WCTU and Washington Equal Suffrage Association—hit Seattle streets with a lead editorial, "Reasons Why You Should Vote for Prohibition" which advised: "If you are ashamed of the bloated faced staggering drunkards along our streets every day . . . vote for prohibition. If you are ashamed of the bloated, loud-mouthed saloon keeper or his patron [who] works for the whisky candidate at your polling place . . . If you would save your boy and your neighbor's boy from becoming a drunkard, vote for prohibition."

Both suffrage and prohibition were defeated by a margin

of more than two to one. The *Leader* haughtily dismissed the ballot-box results with:

By votes we run the devil's still,
By votes we kill God's living grain,
By votes the drunkard's cup we fill
And doom him to eternal pain!

Pointing accusatory fingers at those they felt responsible for their defeat (anyone who did not vote for prohibition), the *Leader* asked, "Who casts these votes? Thou, voter, thou!"

After brushing off warnings not to speak in Almira, Washington, Sutton became, in a very painful way, a casualty of prohibition's struggle. Following Sutton's address, a saloon keeper in the town beat him so severely he was bedridden for three weeks. Supporters presented him with a heavy gold-headed cane, not only to assist the injured prohibitionist in getting about, but also for defence against further physical attacks. The whisky fighter began signing his letters, "Yours for the war, E.B. Sutton."

Against all odds, the increasingly strident WSTA and the "Prohib politicians" railed on. As prohibitionists and their campaigners became more frequently perceived as extremists, much-needed support began to fall away. By the late 1890s, the Pacific Northwest temperance fires that had briefly burned so brightly were reduced to half-dead embers. It would be two decades before the tireless agitation of reform would fan those embers into flames again.

In nearby BC, there was nothing to compare with America's Anti-Saloon League. Nor was there that great groundswell of anti-saloon sentiment that swept the Canadian prairies, finding expression in the church-led Banish the Bar Crusade. Some American and Canadian temperance groups formed alliances with women's suffrage organizations, attacking drink indirectly through a wider social mandate to improve the lives of women. After all, they postulated, who was more adversely affected by men's drunkenness than wives and mothers? Instead of the vehement outrage of Washington and Oregon, however, the BC reform movement, in the guise of either temperance or suffrage, was greeted with polite, paternal condescension.

In 1871, American suffrage leader Susan B. Anthony ventured across the border with Oregon firebrand Abigail Scott Duniway to lecture on women's enfranchisement. Nobody threw rocks, but the two women found the thin smiles and hollow platitudes discouraging just the same. In Victoria, they stared out at an audience of mostly men. A male-dominated audience was no surprise in the small frontier towns they visited in their Pacific Northwest circuit, where fishing, mining and logging demanded brute strength and stamina; however, Victoria was a capital city of about 3,200 people and a centre of some refinement. Where were the ladies to whom their appeals were usually directed?

And the size of the audience was disappointing. There was just a fraction of the 1,000 people (attracted, admittedly, by the Oregon State Fair) the two had addressed late that summer in the state capital, Salem, a smaller city than Victoria.

Duniway concluded that in Canada's newest province, "the ballot for woman was even more unpopular than in the United States." As Anthony and Duniway came, spoke and caused barely a ripple, the irony of the repressive attitude in a city "belonging to a woman's [Queen Victoria's] government" was certainly not lost on the visiting lecturers.

The next years were full of reformist challenges, but BC seemed immune to the incoming tide of change. Idaho women were voting in 1896. Washington women won a lasting franchise by 1910. Oregon women were in the polling booths by 1912. However, in BC, the last western provincial holdout, women did not win the right to vote until 1917, two years after Duniway's death.

Twelve years after the suffragettes' fruitless visit to Victoria, America's foremost temperance leader accepted an invitation to appear north of the border as part of her swing through the Pacific Northwest. Francis Willard, the national president of the WCTU, steamed across Juan de Fuca Strait to attend a provincial temperance convention and make a public address. Willard was to speak at the cathedral-like Metropolitan United Church, which was located not far from the Pandora Avenue brothels and Johnson Street dance halls where liquor ran like water.

Saturday night was a tough night to fill a church for any reason. Diminutive, bespectacled Willard not only had to compete with the noisy conviviality offered by every saloon and restaurant in the city, but on this particular Saturday night, she was in competition with "The Greatest Hit of the Season," Courtright and Hawkins' Minstrels, onstage at the Philharmonic Hall. Nevertheless, Victoria organizers managed to fill the pews with the help of out-of-town delegates who had already begun to arrive for the convention.

Above the floral bowers, the British and American flags and a placard bearing the optimistic motto "O, haste, we pray, the Glorious Day when temperance rules the world," special guests sat looking out at the audience. Among them was the city's mayor, various men of the cloth and MLA John Robson. In an earlier life, Robson, the rabble-rousing editor of New Westminster's *British Columbian*, had been an anomaly amongst his hard-drinking newspaper peers. The brother of Methodist missionary Reverend Ebenezer Robson, the future premier was—at least publicly—a teetotaler. Now he publicly congratulate Miss Willard in having "risen above national lines and come across to assist British Columbians in putting down the monster."

The *Daily Colonist* reported that when Willard spoke passionately of "the hideous affects of drink, she moved the audience almost to tears." However, the story's placement on the third page of the four-page newspaper with no accompanying editorial reflected the near-trivial, chiefly feminine interest in the temperance leader's visit and the convention of a new and untested provincial organization.

Willard's appearance had little effect on the organization's future in BC. While the WCTU was a powerful engine of US reform, development of British Columbia chapters sputtered and stalled. The following year, membership in Victoria—population 12,000—was a mere 236 individuals. In 1893, what organizers claimed was "the largest, most important women's meeting ever held in B.C." drew fewer than 100 delegates.

How different it all was in America's Pacific Northwest! Two years before, Oregon had claimed 83 WCTU chapters with a combined state membership of over 2,000. While the WCTU did achieve some success in BC, the American Anti-Saloon League never established any following whatsoever. The BC public's attitude appeared to be, "The saloon should stay."

WCTU's "sober and pure world" would not be realized—potentially, at least—until individual Canadian provinces went dry during the First World War and the US Constitution's 18th Amendment ratified nationwide American prohibition in 1920. Prohibition represented the most radical social change in both American and Canadian history, and when it finally occurred in the Pacific Northwest, the once-mighty WCTU could claim only partial credit for its enactment. It was the Anti-Saloon League that led the 20th century's temperance-to-prohibition crusade.

CHAPTER

7

Defeats and Victories

EVERY DAY FOR SIX WEEKS at the end of 1908, tens of thousands of Spokane residents—35,000 in one day alone— filed into a specially built wooden "tabernacle" to hear baseball-player-turned-evangelist Reverend Billy Sunday.

"Who makes the money?" Sunday rhetorically asked another overflow crowd. "The dirty gangs of saloon keepers and the brewers and the distillers," he thundered, "and that is the gang that fills the land with misery and poverty and wretchedness!"

It was still many years before Sunday's showmanship and fiery rhetoric would make him a household name from coast to coast. However, by 1908, after almost a decade of saving souls, Sunday and his wife Nell, who had recently become his full-time evangelical manager, were ready for the big time. Sunday recognized an opportunity when he saw it. West Coast ferment created the perfect launch for Sunday's ascent to nationwide notoriety.

Promotion of a "men only" revival meeting drew a noisy throng of 15,000 and "nearly caused a riot," the *Spokesman Review* reported breathlessly the next day. Afterward, Sunday hopped aboard a chartered rail coach bound, if not for Glory, then certainly Olympia, where he was to spread his gospel against "plain devilism" and lobby, in typical stentorian style, for the local option bill. As the train click-clacked west, he rallied the righteous against wicked acts, which also included card playing and dancing, by leading 100 Spokane temperance advocates in prayer.

The day Sunday's train pulled out, the *Spokesman Review*'s eye-grabbing headline, "Beer Sales Fall; Bibles In Demand," was more wishful thinking than fact. The man destined to become the most famous American evangelist in the early 20th century had as much lasting influence on the habits and behaviours of the crowds filling tabernacle seats as Frances Willard had a quarter of a century earlier, when she spoke in Victoria. Just 200 of the thousands who clamoured for admittance to Sunday's men-only meeting actually came forward to "get on the water wagon." Schade Brewery officials shrugged; beer sales were always slow in February. Jacob "Dutch Jake" Goetz's enormous casino and saloon opened a few months later inside his new Coeur d'Alene Hotel and did a rip-roaring trade, as did Jimmie Durkin's three saloons.

Local-option agitation south of the line may have encouraged BC temperance advocates to focus their efforts in the same direction. The provincial WCTU formed a Local Option League, headed by E.B. Morgan, a Vancouver businessman and prominent Methodist. The league invoked the Dominion's 1878 Scott Act, which gave cities and counties the option to prohibit liquor sales if a majority of residents voted in favour of the measure. All provinces except BC already had such laws. It is easy to understand why: local option allowed provincial governments to toss a political hot potato into the hands of local governments, while seeming to acknowledge the democratic principle of allowing the people—not bureaucrats—to decide liquor's fate. The BC government might have done the same if it wasn't for the province's self-centred, patronage-loving premier, Richard McBride.

Since 1903, the outwardly charming, witty premier and his Attorney General, William (Billy) Bowser, had constructed an unprecedented political machine. McBride detested the Local Option League, which he regarded as a direct threat to his power base. His concern must have deepened in 1909 as 50 local delegates attended the league's surprisingly large provincial convention in Vancouver.

McBride had a lot riding on the status quo. In a number of Tory ridings, some very influential politicos just happened

British Columbia premier Richard McBride loathed reformers generally, but especially prohibitionists. Ever the opportunist, McBride was good at knowing which way the political and social winds were blowing.

to be liquor-industry leaders. Liquor licensing had become a patronage plum; through the government-appointed Board of License Commissioners, the government had the power to grant or rescind licences. Allowing voters to force local governments to shut down the revenue-producing, patronage-rewarding industry was not on McBride's agenda.

The term "patronage" was not yet burdened with its later connotation of corruption. For more than a century, patronage was considered, by all levels of government, an appropriate reward for hard work and valuable services rendered. During the McBride era, a group of influential gents, quite openly referred to as the "patronage committee," determined who received plum positions and just what those positions might be.

On the eve of a provincial election, McBride was presented with an anti-liquor petition of over 35,000 signatures, 10,000 of which belonged to eligible voters. Smiling all the while, the premier quickly promised a plebiscite on the issue in the upcoming provincial election. But the fix was in.

The government decreed that a local-option victory would be based not on a majority of those who voted on the issue, but a majority of all the voters who cast ballots in the election. Local Option League members screamed foul, but it didn't matter. Once ballots were counted, the re-elected government declared local option defeated. The real reason, the Local Option League discovered sometime later, was that the government hadn't printed enough local-option ballots to begin with. The premier attempted to keep the prohibition wolves at bay by enforcing a strict Sunday closing law on saloons, and in 1911, bringing an end to American-style free-standing saloons. The government decreed that saloon owners must convert their premises to hotels by 1914.

Despite these superficial changes, reformers knew that it was business as usual for BC's booze industry, and soon it was business as usual for the Conservative government as well. In the provincial election of 1912, the Liberals, who supported women's suffrage and local-option laws, went down to a humiliating defeat. Voters handed Richard McBride a landslide victory. The electorate (all men at this point) had spoken: the saloon could stay and so could the reigning provincial government.

While BC's Local Option League had been preparing for its 1909 Vancouver convention, the local-option struggle consumed Washington State, where the Anti-Saloon League led prohibition forces into battle. Walla Walla, the state's newest incorporated city, was the first major centre to present local-option petitions to legislators. With 37 saloons doing business in a city of 15,000 and with the wets led by a notable banker and businessman, the petition obviously didn't represent everyone's views.

Some of the strongest local-option support came from rural residents. Many in Walla Walla County had repeatedly petitioned for Sunday saloon closures, at the very least. When farmhands left for a city visit, their frustrated farmer-employers never knew if they would return, or, if they did, if they would be in any condition to work. The temptations of big-city saloons threatened every farm family's future harvest and livelihood.

As elections loomed, farmers drove their wagons to Walla Walla to crusade against its saloons. There were demonstrations and fist fights throughout the business district for a full week before polls opened. A long letter from Governor Marion Hay, describing saloons as a "cancer," was read out to the crowds during a climactic dry rally. Nevertheless, when the ballots were counted, Walla Walla stayed wet, 1,630 to 1,008.

The following year, wet-dry tensions divided the hard-working, hard-drinking mill town of Everett (which proudly proclaimed itself the "City of Smokestacks"), where 40 saloons lined Hewitt Avenue. The anti-saloon faction invited Billy Sunday to pontificate. The saloon operators enlisted the help of legendary criminal lawyer Clarence Darrow, who spoke in defence of personal liberty. Once again, wets and drys fought each other in the streets. After Sunday church services, 2,500 children marched through the city, bearing banners that read "repent ye boozers" and "the saloon must go." Then came victory! The men of Everett voted dry, 2,208 to 1,933. On the same day, the city of Bellingham, north of Everett, also voted to close its saloons.

However, state legislators rebuked the ASL because its local-option fight "had cut wounds that affected public interest." After a rancorous day-long debate, Governor Hay was stunned when the legislature resolved not to hear any proposed liquor legislation in 1911, when Hay had planned to support the introduction of county local options. The ASL then switched tactics, endorsing "I and R" (initiative and referendum) direct legislation and forming a Direct Legislation League to help turn wet counties dry. They weren't alone. Oregon prohibitionists were proposing direct legislation, too. But they had a more ambitious end in mind: statewide prohibition.

The early 1890s had been hard years for most residents of Pacific coast states and almost everywhere else in America. Rumour had it that the US gold supply was a lot smaller than most thought. Overbuilt railroads, which relied on this supply, began to collapse, leading to a series of bank failures. Before long, BC residents felt the economic domino effect. In 1894, Vancouver churches were feeding hundreds of hungry residents daily. In coastal Washington State, so many were reduced to digging up waterfront clams to feed their families that a Tacoma congressman commented that "their stomachs rose and fell with the tide."

However, during the summer of 1897, the slight upward curve of coastal prosperity became much steeper, literally overnight, when dozens of Yukon gold-creek millionaires disembarked from the "treasure ships" *Excelsior* and

Portland. Caught up in the excitement, Seattle welcomed not only those returning south who had already "made their pile," but thousands of would-be stampeders from the east. Seattle rooming houses and hotels were crammed, and restaurants ran out of food while men in long lines waited impatiently for a seat at their tables. Retailers who stocked frontier clothing and tools were desperate to fill empty shelves. A few months later, the onset of the Spanish-American War also boosted coastal business.

Consequently, as the new century dawned, life was better for most. Residents and newcomers alike celebrated in typical fashion: they drank. By then, Seattle was a divided city. The phrases "open town" and "closed town" soon defined the schism within city boundaries. "Open town" meant one that put profits from restricted and regulated drinking, gambling and prostitution first; "closed-town" meant one that reflected reform and moral restraint. Seattle residents could see evidence of the divide plainly enough. By 1908, Seattle would boast about 100 churches and 211 saloons. Seattle's bright, shiny new prosperity came with an ugly underside of vice and corruption.

Former lawyer and judge Thomas Humes was Seattle's mayor from 1897 to 1904. With his flowing white moustache and head of wavy silver hair, Humes resembled a West Coast Mark Twain. The resemblance ended there. Humes was an open-town man, a true friend of those on the seamy side. In Humes's Seattle, men toting nuggets and fingering folding money had plenty of places to part with it, including saloons, gambling casinos and brothels.

Gambling was officially shut down for a short while in the spring of 1899, but nothing changed. Drinks continued to be poured, cards were dealt, roulette wheels spun and men paid for female "companionship." Casino owners met to formalize the sector's rules of operation, which included, as Rule Number Five, "Police to notify when fines are due." The "fines" were routine, and casino owners simply regarded them as the cost of doing a very good business. It is possible that they were actually look-the-other-way bribes. The relationship between the police and casino owners was very cosy; in fact, the chosen location for the owners' meeting was the office of Police Chief Charles S. Reed.

The town's wide-open reputation spread. A notorious Wild West gambling house and saloon owner arrived to investigate a start-up in Seattle. His future competitors informed him that before he opened he had to check in with Chief Reed. Frontier legend Wyatt Earp guessed why. "You fellows are paying enough," the survivor of the Gunfight at the OK Corral chuckled. "Why should I add any money?" He didn't, at least not initially, and opened the Union Club Betting Parlour and Saloon anyway.

"Boss Sport" John Considine, one of Earp's competitors, had been handing money to the police for years. The city's "barmaid" ordinance had banned female employment where alcohol was served. Bags of police payoff money kept the ladies at work at Considine's People's Theatre, a box-house saloon where free-spending Yukon prospectors rented semi-private boxes to watch women entertain and serve drinks as a prelude to more intimate "entertainment." Before long, Earp and his partner were paying the customary fines, too, including a December 1899 payment of $175, based on five games.

Chief Reed's successor was closed-town man William Meredith. Tensions rose. In 1901, John Considine publicly disclosed that police had approached a city-council committee in search of payoff money. The casino operator's scheme worked: Chief Meredith was forced to resign from office. Then things got personal. Conniving Considine revealed that Meredith had impregnated a saloon entertainer, a contortionist named Mamie Jenkins.

A sawed-off shotgun concealed beneath his coat, vengeful Meredith shadowed John Considine around the city and watched him and his brother Tom saunter into a drugstore. Meredith followed, pointed the shotgun and fired. Unfortunately, the spray of shot hit an innocent youngster at the soda-fountain counter and merely wounded John. Coming to his brother's rescue, unarmed Tom flew at Meredith. In the desperate struggle that followed, Tom managed to fracture Meredith's skull. Bleeding and cursing, John pulled his .38 and shot the former chief three times as he lay semi-conscious on the drugstore's floor tiles. At Considine's murder trial, the jury returned a not guilty verdict; the casino kingpin had obviously shot in self-defence during a "continuous struggle."

It might have been a new century, but old 19th-century attitudes lingered. It was a bad time to be a closed-town advocate. Nevertheless, there were plenty of them in the city, although none held office or even aspired to do so. What these advocates held, instead, were demonstrations. One of the most spectacular occurred in April 1905. On that day, the Salvation Army Band led 15,000 crusaders, including white-haired seniors and little children, through streets where few of them had ventured before, south of Yesler Way and past the red-light district's saloons, brothels, gambling dens and dance halls.

Police payoffs continued under two terms of Police Chief Charles "Wappy" Wappenstein, the walrus-mustachioed little dandy who had once assisted William Meredith in his fight against graft and done the same during the closed-town term of Mayor William Moore. When Moore was defeated by the city's most notorious open-towner, Hiram Gill, Wappy deftly switched sides and flourished as Gill's chief. Wappenstein personally informed madams of the Midway, Paris and other newly reopened brothels that the cost of remaining in business was $10 per girl per month, payable to him or his officers. In a city of over 500 prostitutes, that represented quite a haul. Seattle's "tenderloin" area south of Yesler Way was soon dubbed "Wappyville."

Candidate Gill had promised voters that the red-light

Charles "Wappy" Wappenstein, Seattle
police chief and one of the city's best-
known pre-Prohibition figures, adroitly
played both sides for his own gain
during the city's booze-and-brothels
battles. UNIVERSITY OF WASHINGTON LIBRARIES,
SPECIAL COLLECTIONS UW27558Z

district would be "the most quiet place in Seattle . . . men will have to go out of their way to find it." It didn't work out that way, of course. Throughout the city, Lady Luck continued to lure men not only into saloons and casinos, but into cigar stores and barbershops that operated profitable gambling sidelines. Incensed members of Seattle's reformist organizations watched construction crews building a 500-room brothel, which held a 15-year lease from the city itself.

Then, in 1911, through investigative journalists at the *Seattle Post-Intelligencer* and the tireless efforts of suffragettes, Seattle's closed-town and reform advocates won a pair of stunning victories. Women celebrated both. The first came when Washington women won the right to vote. Shocked by the *Post-Intelligencer*'s revelations of civic corruption, Seattle residents petitioned for a recall election. In the second victory, 20,000 of the city's 23,000 registered women voters cast ballots and helped throw Gill out of office and elect closed-towner and local-option, temperance and suffrage supporter George Dilling.

Eventually, Wappy Wappenstein was sentenced to a stretch in Walla Walla's state penitentiary, but it wasn't easy to put him there. It took the talents of sleuths working for the William Burns Detective Agency to provide the evidence needed to arrest Wappy and spark the recall of Mayor Gill. Yet, just a few years later, in the aftermath of the state's final whisky wars, Hiram Gill made an astonishing comeback, landing a starring role on the Seattle political stage.

8

Dry at Last

OSCAR LARSEN NEEDED A BOTTLE and he needed it badly. Despite his inebriated state, he knew exactly where to go. Larsen stumbled toward the liquor store near the corner of Powell Street and Hawkes Avenue, not far from his shack on Vancouver's Burrard Inlet. Inside the store, personnel took one look at the bleary-eyed drunk weaving his way to the counter and knowingly rolled their eyes. Their nonchalance vanished when Larsen began terrorizing customers with a .38-calibre revolver. Proprietor John MacRea asked the telephone operator to put him through to police.

Under the date March 25, 1912, the desk sergeant scratched out the terse notation, "Drunk, annoying." He summoned fresh-faced, clean-shaven constable Lewis Byers, who was puzzled. Somebody actually telephoned about a drunk? Times were good; dozens of hotel bars did a roaring business, and people were continually sidestepping tipsy patrons. The annoying thing was the telephone call itself. When the sergeant said a Swede—it sounded like Oscar Larsen, who had been hauled in by police before—had pulled a gun, the constable understood why he had been ordered to arrest the guy. This sounded more like an attempted robbery than a drunk-and-disorderly.

The store was too far from the station for Byers to simply walk there. Options were limited. True, automobiles had just been purchased for the police chief and the detective squad, but even if these exciting new "motors" had already been delivered, Byers wasn't going to get to use one. The constable left on foot, headed for the nearest eastbound streetcar.

The policeman's stop at the store was short. Nobody had been shot, thankfully. Gun in hand, the drunk had simply backed through the front door and disappeared. Employees thought they knew where Byers could find him. When Byers reached the waterfront and looked about, he wondered which one of the tin-roofed shacks belonged to the suspect. He didn't have to wonder long.

Just five yards away, a door jerked open and Larsen lurched out, pointing his revolver. Reaching for his own side-arm, Byers stepped quickly towards cover—but not quickly enough. Larsen fired again and watched the cop tumble to the ground, blood running from his chest and neck.

Witnesses called in the shooting, and Detective Crew and a constable responded. They found ambulance attendants crouched down behind the wheel of their vehicle. Within moments, they were crouching, too. Through his door, Larsen was blasting away in all directions. Other officers arrived on the scene within a few minutes, and under covering fire, Crew managed to drag Byers to safety.

"We riddled the shack with bullets as the man inside continued firing," Crew reported. Abruptly, the shooting from the shack stopped. A constable cautiously crept forward and opened the door. Inside, police found Larsen "lying on his side, apparently shot in the chest and neck during our volley." Wounded by a combination of police fire and self-inflicted gunshots, the Swede would not live out the night. Lewis Byers was dead before he reached the hospital.

"Sorrowing Thousands View Somber Pageant," the *Vancouver Daily World*'s front page announced six days later. Hastings Street crowds looked on at Byer's lengthy funeral procession, which included three bands, contingents of Boy Scouts, Highland militia, the IODE, police, firemen, mail carriers and "the lonely figure of the young wife . . . weeping bitterly in a carriage behind the hearse." Young Vancouver had never seen a spectacle like it.

Speaking inside the Central Methodist Church, Reverend R.J. Wilson hinted at those responsible for Byer's death. He didn't point his finger at "the poor drunk-crazed fool" who had pulled the trigger. He pointed it at those who gave the "wretched man . . . such quantities of liquor that would rob any man of his senses." Drunken binges could turn deadly, and Wilson admonished, "It should be made impossible for such a thing to be tolerated in such a decent city."

However, Vancouver's emotionally charged, quasi-military tribute hadn't been staged because West Coast whisky wars had taken two more lives, but simply because Lewis Byers just happened to be the city's very first police officer killed in the line of duty. Displayed on an inside page of the *Vancouver Daily World* was a photograph of the horse-drawn hearse carrying Byer's remains. Directly opposite the photo was a large ad for that "royal drink," King George IV Liqueur Whisky.

BC's good times would not last long. By 1913, sliding commodity prices meant economic death for the fishing, logging and mining province. The only economic statistic on the upswing was unemployment. The most severe labour unrest in the province's history jolted Vancouver Island and the Kootenays as coal miners walked away from slave-wage collieries. "Bowser's Bulldogs," the Attorney General's tough special constables, went to work on the strikers. Their arrival in Nanaimo sparked a riot during which a constable was shot and a chief of police stoned. Twelve hundred soldiers were sent in, and hundreds were arrested.

The government's previous expansionist program, so promising in a buoyant economy, weighed the province down even further. It was bad enough that the new, costly Canadian Northern Pacific and Pacific Great Eastern railroads were still unprofitable, but the tens of millions of dollars borrowed for their development were still outstanding. Then, the First World War erupted.

The unemployed had already been taking ships and trains out of the province, headed for more promising horizons. Now, able-bodied employees walked off their jobs and onto trains and ships, wearing new uniforms. By war's end, almost 10 percent of the province's population wore khaki, most serving overseas and unable to contribute to their province's economy. In late 1915, BC residents were stunned when the premier also suddenly quit his job and sailed for England. Speculation ran wild: McBride had left to avoid a secret scandal; ambitious Bowser was blackmailing him; McBride's master plan was to rise in the federal government; or—two years later on his death from Bright's Disease—McBride had known he was dying. McBride had actually accepted another job, becoming agent general in London's BC House. Reluctantly, Billy Bowser also took on another position. The former Attorney General became acting premier.

All of these bleak developments didn't have everyone frowning. Opportunistic suffragettes and temperance-cum-prohibition advocates were privately pleased with the province's turn of events. So were BC's beleaguered Liberals and their new leader, Baptist cannery owner and millionaire Harlan Brewster.

On the other side of the 49th parallel, the hard work by Washington State's Anti-Saloon League had led to some

Huge crowds of spectators strain behind rope barriers as "drys" march in Seattle in 1911, a testimony to reform's influence. North of the border, where BC residents gave prohibitionists and suffragettes alike a cold shoulder, such demonstrations were rare.

WASHINGTON STATE HISTORICAL SOCIETY, WSHS#1999.63.2.25

success, despite the 1912 electoral defeat of its champion, Governor Hay. The year women finally entered polling stations, initiative and referendum proposals passed easily. The league's calculations revealed Washington's dry areas included 42 percent of the state's population. Bellingham had remained dry, and six counties were dry. With the exception of Everett, votes indicated strong anti-saloon sentiments. In Oregon, prohibitionists' hopes soared. While it was true that state voters had narrowly voted down a prohibition referendum two years before, women now had the vote. That meant bad news for wets and good news for drys.

In Washington State, a series of ASL-led initiatives were undertaken, organized through churches and spearheaded by signed petitions. After years of resolute, step-by-step efforts, Initiative Number 3 was introduced and success seemed within the prohibitionists' grasp. Although it garnered no headlines, one of the reasons for the eventual swing to prohibition was the mindset of many younger voters.

In one of their most strategic endeavours, Washington prohibitionists had successfully pressured the Territorial Assembly to pass the Alcohol Education Act in 1886, which required that public schools teach students about the effects of liquor. The instruments of the sometimes-overcharged instruction—just one drink was enough to make you a drunk!—were schoolteachers, who enjoyed a high level of influence. Having been formally indoctrinated against drink in their childhood, thousands of voters were ready to mark their ballot for prohibition.

More people could now read, and what some were reading were new myth-shattering scientific and medical findings: alcohol was a depressant, not a stimulant; it constricted blood vessels so could not actually warm the body; it impaired mental activity, lowered resistance to disease and was injurious to kidneys and liver. These disclosures provided more ammunition for prohibitionists.

The ASL focused their energies on influencing Seattle's

tolerant, urban residents, who leaned toward the wet side. If they could convince enough city folk to vote dry, these numbers, coupled with the expected high number of dry rural votes, would tip the balance. As the wets' campaign ramped up, Seattle chamber of commerce members voted solidly against Initiative Number 3 by 632 to 45 votes. Number 3 was a "nauseous dose," sneered *Seattle Times* editor Alden Blethen, and Seattle didn't need to swallow it. For Blethen, statewide prohibition would be a "calamity."

The men who ran the city's more sophisticated journals were against the ASL initiative on an economic level. In the words of the *Town Crier*, Number 3 was "simply and entirely destructive of existing property rights and the revenues upon which state, county, city and school district now depend." In a statement that would later haunt Americans everywhere, the editor of the clear-eyed *Argus* warned that while there was no good argument for selling liquor, "it is better to have it sold legally than illegally." Brewery barons placed full-page ads urging "moderation but not prohibition." Fearing lost jobs if Number 3 became law, union locals representing bartenders, cooks, waiters, musicians and even cigar-makers formed the Anti-Prohibition Labor League to fight the measure.

Having circulated the petitions for signatures, churches galvanized for action. Presbyterians contributed $150,000 for the coming campaign in four states, including Oregon and Washington. Methodists sent hundreds of ministers into communities to spread the dry gospel. The Presbyterian

Church sent the lean, six-foot-five "Black-Maned Lion," Reverend Mark Matthews, whose First Presbyterian Church served a congregation of 3,000. "Few men can paint black blacker than he," *Colliers: The National Weekly* told its huge readership, and he did it with "smashing similes that stick and scald and burn." To Matthews, the saloon was "the most fiendish, corrupt and hell-soaked institution that ever crawled out of the slime of the eternal pit." The country's leaders weren't much better, Matthews told his faithful. "The two great political parties are rum-soaked, saloon-cursed and without conscience on the question of the abolition of this great enemy."

The ASL dug down into the grassroots, organizing Washington State into hundreds of precincts and appointing captains in each one to oversee door-to-door canvassers. As the campaign reached a near-frenzy at the end of October, residents erected billboards in front yards, singers and speakers attracted huge audiences, autos and brass bands paraded through the streets, and hundreds of teenagers marched in after-dark torchlight processions.

Prohibition managed to win over just 39 percent of Seattle's voters and trailed in Washington's second- and third-largest cities, Spokane and Tacoma. It did not matter. As prohibition strategists had hoped, rural voters—and those in Everett and Bellingham—carried the day. The initiative passed by a statewide total of 189,840 to 171,208 votes. With the exception of liquor importation and sale for medicinal purposes, Washington State would go dry on January 1, 1916. Oregon went one step further: on the same day, it would go "bone-dry," allowing no liquor exceptions at all.

The law spelled the end for liquor men. Until the dry date arrived, many carried on as if nothing would change—but not Spokane's Jimmie Durkin. Boldly announcing, "I and my organization will give the law the strictest obedience," he then used prohibition as a once-in-a-lifetime business promotion. Durkin organized a gigantic closing-out sale. Week after week, under the headline, "Durkin's—Be in at the Death," ads proclaimed low, low prices at "a bargain table of imported and domestic liquors and wines" prominently positioned inside each of his three saloons (or stores, as he preferred to call them). A newspaper article about Durkin's closures listed a huge inventory that included (as Durkin's ads boasted), "more whiskies . . . than any three wholesale dealers on the Pacific Coast, except Craig of San Francisco." The sale began in July 1915 and went on, month after month, until Washington State's last wet days.

As the dry date approached, various efforts were made either to kill Number 3 or amend it, but Governor Ernest Lister made it clear that he would use his veto to defeat any such wet move. Another initiative, Number 18, was designed to amend the prohibition law to permit the sale of liquor in hotels. The Grange, a well-established rural temperance organization, attacked Number 18 as an attempt to "make the saloon . . . a brothel of the hotels of the land."

Cowed legislators banished the measure to committee. It never returned to the floor.

Washington and Oregon's contentious whisky wars paled in comparison to the larger war BC's Expeditionary Force volunteers had been waging. By mid-1915, the news from the front of choking poison gas at Ypres was horrific. Thousands of BC men had already died or were horribly maimed. Despairing folks back home felt impotent; their fighting men were making terrible sacrifices. Shouldn't friends and families make a sacrifice, too? prohibitionists asked, conveniently ignoring the sacrifices already made by suddenly widowed women and bereft parents whose husbands and sons had fallen in the mud of no-man's land. And so, in the most bizarre example of social manipulation in Canada's short history, residents of BC—and elsewhere— were persuaded to sacrifice the freedom to enjoy a drink.

Prohibitionists' overt rationales were economic ones. Hangovers reduced the efficiency of workers in war industries, the very industries that needed men who were still tending bar, distilling booze and brewing beer. And grain was needed for vital foodstuffs, not alcoholic beverages. But most of these were specious arguments, at best. While hangovers may have kept some men from working, prohibition was a poor strategy to fill vacancies in war-industry plants. If a government wartime subsidy had boosted factory-workers' pay, many barkeeps and labourers would have abandoned lower-paying jobs in saloons and breweries and in other sectors, as well. There is no evidence that the amount of grain used for brewing and distilling would have resulted in food shortages or rationing, in spite of the urgings of the Canada Food Board to conserve wheat and sugar.

Besides, most of the food in question would have been consumed in Canada, not in Flanders. If men in the trenches went hungry from time to time, it was likely due to battlefield conditions and the logistical nightmares of transporting supplies behind the lines.

BC prohibitionists began consolidating their forces in May 1915. At a huge banquet in Vancouver's Dominion Hall, over 500 of the city's businessmen and professional men unanimously endorsed provincial prohibition. Attendees also endorsed a proposal that insurance agent D.F. Glass travel throughout the province to request the support of businessmen for prohibition.

In late August, a Vancouver-based People's Prohibition Association (PPA) organized and hosted a two-day convention that attracted many of the prohibition-minded people Glass had spoken to in the interior. McBride sensed trouble. In an effort to head it off, the day before the convention commenced, the premier wrote to the convention committee that the government had decided, "after careful deliberation to submit the whole question to a plebiscite of the electorate."

The convention's climactic moment came at its public rally. An audience of 4,000 heard the fiery oration of noted prairie suffrage and prohibition crusader Nellie McClung, among others. In a particularly zealous moment, McClung rationalized Flanders field's carnage, declaring that "without shedding of blood, there is no remission of sin."

While McBride's offer of a plebiscite fell short of pro-hibitionists' objective of obtaining a legally binding referendum, the significance of his letter was obvious: if the nascent group could provoke such a swift, personal response from the province's premier, what might they achieve if it enjoyed province-wide support? Consequently, one of the most important outcomes of the convention was the decision to reach out, through delegates, to make the PPA a provincial organization complete with "locals" in towns and villages everywhere. By the new year, the PPA's first president, Vancouver builder Jonathan Rogers, claimed that there were prohibition committees in all but 2 of 30 electoral districts.

The PPA's boast appears more meaningful than it really was. All prohibitionists had to do was capture Vancouver and Victoria in a substantial way and they could carry the day. The two largest cities represented over half the prov-ince's population. The issue never pitted "country folk" against "city folk" either, because wartime prohibition was popular almost everywhere. The situation was different in Washington State, and to some degree in Oregon. Seattle and Spokane represented less than a third of Washington's population. The ASL and WCTU were desperate to reach out to rural voters, and without a wartime rationale, getting prohibition passed was more of a challenge.

In the late summer of 1916, as its prohibition campaign intensified, the PPA made an exciting announcement: North America's best-known dry speaker was bringing his captivating anti-saloon message to both Vancouver and Victoria. The Reverend Billy Sunday was on his way! It had been an exhilarating journey for Sunday since 1908, when he attracted 30,000 people during his Spokane triumph. By now, Sunday's popularity was nearing its peak; he was building "tabernacles" in some of America's biggest cities. He routinely spoke to crowds of tens of thousands, and his followers numbered in the millions. He did not disappoint. The saloon, he shouted to 12,000 Vancouverites who sat before him, "is God's worst enemy and hell's best friend." Inside Victoria's hockey arena he exhorted, "If the saloon is not the dirtiest thing on God's earth, the devil ought to be canonized."

What was disappointing to the PPA was that, aside from laudatory coverage in the *Vancouver Daily World*, Sunday failed to impress the media. The *News-Advertiser* shrugged that Sunday did "not prove a sensation." Scoffing that three-quarters of the audience were women, Labour's *Federationist* labelled him a tool of capitalists (perhaps because Sunday was against government regulation of anything beside liquor). The *Federationist*'s most scathing comments were not directed at the substance of Sunday's oratory, but at his flamboyant style and "automatic mouth":

How I love its giddy gargle
How I love its rhythmic flow
How I love to wind my mouth up,
How I love to hear it go.

How different the attitude was across the border, the PPA must have reflected. Sunday was revered in the US.

Wets, at last, found their voice. Businessmen, including the owner of New Westminster Breweries and the local manager of distillers Hiram Walker & Company, formed the Merchants Protective Association (MPA). The MPA flooded newspapers with ads and editorials, distributed thousands of leaflets and presented the government with a petition bearing over 30,000 names, asking that a liquor vote be postponed until after the war, and—in the awful event prohibition did succeed—that hotels and brewers be compensated.

Using economics as its whisky-war weapon, labour's *B.C. Federationist* editorialized: "If prohibition became law tomorrow in Vancouver, New Westminster and Victoria, would that fact increase the jobs for the unemployed who now abound in each of those cities?" Its answer: "We do not believe it would." Like prohibitionists, wets could talk food, too. Ignoring new medical findings, unions gave beer a healthful, nutritional status. Cumberland mineworkers travelled to Victoria carrying a 6,000-signature petition to keep beer flowing legally. "The average robustness of the British Columbia miner was partly due to reasonable use of beer as a stimulant," union local spokesman Joe Naylor stated. Should some scoff, Naylor assured *Colonist* readers that if it banned suds, the province would face "further Industrial strife."

John Nelson, owner and editor of the *Vancouver Daily World*, turned prohibition propagandist, asking drinkers and non-drinkers alike to unite for the war effort. "No country that is at war has any business permitting the continuance of a trade," Nelson intoned, "which imposes unnecessary burdens on industry and commerce and entails worse ravages than war itself." Nelson, obviously, hadn't been to the western front.

Little wonder that a man standing at a bar might feel a twinge of guilt—as prohibitionists intended—as he gulped down another rye. However, there wasn't much guilt in the rat-infested trenches, where unbeknownst to many back home, thousands of sons, husbands and fathers were gulping down rum. With the ability to numb shredded bodies and sooth shattered nerves, daily rum rations were regarded as medicinal and absolutely vital to morale. Consequently, wet premier Billy Bowser decided to delay most battlefield prohibition balloting until after the province's vote, when overseas results might be manipulated as required.

There was no way Bowser could manipulate the voting back home, though. Under teetotaler Brewster, Liberals (soberly) celebrated a landslide victory. Voters—exclusively men—also made decisions on suffrage and prohibition. Both plebiscites passed; prohibition by a mere few thousand. BC would go dry—if thousands of soldiers overseas agreed.

BC men of the 29th Battalion, Canadian Expeditionary Force, mark ballots at the Somme in 1916, voting not only for a new provincial government, but also on prohibition.

CITY OF VANCOUVER ARCHIVES A31845

Months after balloting, it still wasn't clear which way soldiers had voted. Representatives for both wets and drys had sailed for Europe to advance their respective causes. Some military officers worked hard to get their men to vote wet (one sergeant major raised a toast with his men with the words, "To Hell with Prohibition!").

The man responsible for collecting and counting battlefield ballots was none other than Richard McBride, who announced that only 812 men out of 8,500 had voted dry—nine to one against prohibition. The BC vote had been overturned—or so it seemed. The lopsided result defied belief, and angry prohibitionists besieged the legislature.

In his last days as premier, Bowser was forced to support a commission to investigate.

Working under the Prohibition Overseas Vote Investigation Act, Conservative and Liberal representatives met in London to investigate misconduct, corruption and fraud, working after the fact to reconstruct a definitive voters list. It was an exercise in futility. As many as 5,000 of the 8,500 voters remained untraceable. Hundreds of men appeared to have voted twice, over 2,000 men had voted in the wrong location, and perhaps just as many weren't even BC residents. Over 1,000 names couldn't even be verified as belonging to actual people. To this day, no one knows how many soldiers actually put an x on a ballot.

Military officers, it was discovered, had made it all but impossible for scrutineers to monitor voting. Officers had failed to swear voters as to their residency, and ballots lacked soldiers' all-important identifying military number. Over half of the 8,500 ballots were rejected under the catch-all term "irregularities." Scrutineer W.D. Bayley summed it up: "Do not blame soldiers because of the fictitious ballots or the ballots that were torn up. But we are accusing certain agents of the liquor traffic of plugging [bribing] and robbing the men who have gone overseas to fight for us . . . It is up to us to see that these bloodsuckers of the liquor traffic don't get the chance to bleed our returning soldiers of every cent they have."

To most soldiers' dismay, residents took Bayley's words to heart. Jubilant but weary uniformed men arrived home to a dry province. Thousands of returning soldiers—known ever afterward as veterans—who believed that they richly deserved and, in some cases, needed an occasional drink, found that they were now denied that former right for their own good. BC prohibition had gone into effect on October 1, 1917.

* * *

It had begun as a measure taken to maximize the profits of the fur trade. It was then proclaimed to prevent bloodshed between Natives and whites. Over half a century later, fervent reformers south of the 49th parallel embraced prohibition in their quest for a better world. In Canada, it was transformed into an expression of wartime sacrifice. In the early years of the 20th century, the prohibition of the manufacture, sale and—to a great degree—transport of liquor became both state and provincial law throughout the Pacific Northwest.

This time, prohibition—the most repressive legislation enacted against West Coast residents to that time—had come about not through the dictates of profit-motivated committeemen in a London boardroom, nor by the decree of a territorial or colonial government. The decision to deprive citizens of the right to drink alcoholic beverages had been made democratically, through the ballot box, by the citizens themselves. Yet, in the face of avarice and desire, history had already demonstrated that the law could not be enforced. Once again, it was doomed to fail.

Selected Bibliography

Many books, newspapers, websites and unpublished manuscripts and other documents were consulted in the preparation of this book. The sources listed below were indispensible to its completion. The author extends his appreciation to those who, online and in person, were so helpful, including personnel at the BC Archives, Maritime Museum of BC, Vancouver Police Museum, City of Victoria Archives and many historical bloggers.

Books

Akrigg, G.P.V. and Helen Akrigg. *British Columbia Chronicle 1847–1871: Gold and Colonists.* Vancouver: Discovery Press, 1977.

Campbell, Robert A. *Demon Rum or Easy Money: Government Control of Liquor in British Columbia, from Prohibition to Privatization.* Ottawa: Carlton University Press, 1991.

Clark, Cecil. *B.C. Provincial Police Stories, Volume One: Mystery and Murder from the Files of Western Canada's First Lawmen.* Surrey: Heritage House Publishing Company Ltd., 1999.

———. "Western Canada's Pioneer Lawmen." In *Outlaws and Lawmen of Western Canada, Vol. 2.* Surrey: Heritage House Publishing Company Ltd., 1983.

Clark, Norman H. *The Dry Years: Prohibition and Social Change in Washington.* Seattle: University of Washington Press, 1988.

Gough, Barry M. *Gunboat Frontier: British Maritime Authority and Northwest Coast Indians.* Vancouver: University of British Columbia Press, 1984.

Hamilton, Douglas L. *Sobering Dilemma: A History of Prohibition in British Columbia.* Vancouver: Ronsdale Press, 2004.

Mackie, Richard Somerset. *Trading Beyond the Mountains: The British Fur Trade on the Pacific, 1793–1843*. Vancouver: University of British Columbia Press, 1997.

Newman, Peter C. *Caesars of the Wilderness*. Toronto: Penguin Books, 1987.

———. *Company of Adventurers*. Toronto: Penguin Books, 1985.

Pethick, Derek. *Victoria: The Fort*. Victoria: Mitchell Press, 1968.

Articles

Anderson, Rick. "Excerpts from *Shakedown Streets*." *Seattle Weekly*, October 20, 2010.

Lamb, W.K. "The Discovery of Hill's Bar in 1858." *British Columbia Historical Quarterly* 3 (July 1939): 215–20.

Potter, Pam. "Wyatt Earp in Seattle." *Wild West* 20 (Oct. 2007): 46.

Newspapers

Vancouver Daily World.

Spokesman-Review (Spokane, WA).

Websites

British Colonist. Online edition 1858–1910. University of Victoria digital collections. www.britishcolonist.ca

HistoryLink. www.historylink.org

Vancouver Police Museum. www.vancouverpolicemuseum.ca

Index

About the Author

Rich Mole is a former broadcaster, communications consultant and president of a Vancouver Island advertising agency. Rich lives in Calgary, Alberta, where he continues to research and write popular histories in the Amazing Stories series. Rich's Heritage House books include *Christmas in BC; Christmas in the Prairies, Great Stanley Cup Victories, Against All Odds: The Edmonton Oilers; Gold Fever; Rebel Women of the Gold Rush; Rebel Women of the Pacific Coast; The Chilcotin War, Dirty Thirties Desperadoes* and *Whisky Wars of the Canadian West.*

Rich is currently working on a second book that continues the fascinating story of booze in British Columbia, Washington and Oregon. The dramatic and funny battles for and against prohibition are told through the front-line combatants: ardent prohibitionists, beleaguered politicians, overwhelmed police officers, entrepreneurial booze barons and intrepid coastal rumrunners, whose legacies continue to affect our 21st-century lives. The new book will also reveal why two peoples, peacefully sharing a coastline, some living just few miles from each other, remain—as far as liquor is concerned—worlds apart.

Rich may be contacted at ramole@telus.net.

More Amazing Stories by Rich Mole

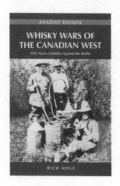

Whisky Wars of the Canadian West
Fifty Years of Battles Against the Bottle

print ISBN 978-1-926613-93-2
ebook ISBN 978-1-926936-99-4

In 1874, the North West Mounted Police marched west to shut down unscrupulous liquor traders. Their trek heralded over 50 years of "whisky wars" in western Canada. Here are the stories of those who suffered and profited from the West's insatiable thirst for liquor. From whisky traders and bootleggers .to temperance movements and prohibition, this is a fascinating account of a turbulent era.

Dirty Thirties Desperadoes
Forgotten Victims of the Great Depression

print ISBN 978-1-926613-95-6
ebook ISBN 978-1-926936-64-2

In October 1935, three Doukhobor farm boys embarked on a violent trail of robbery and murder that stretched from Manitoba to Alberta. By the time the spree ended, the fugitives and four lawmen were dead. This gripping narrative reveals surprising new details about the tragic events as it chronicles the disastrous impact of the Great Depression on the young killers and those who faced them down.

Purchase Amazing Stories at your favourite bookstore or visit heritagehouse.ca to order online.

More Amazing Stories by Rich Mole

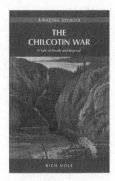

The Chilcotin War
A Tale of Death and Reprisal

print ISBN 978-1-894974-96-7
ebook ISBN 978-1-926936-30-7

In 1864, a Tsilhqot'in war party killed members of a road crew carving out a mountain shortcut to the Cariboo gold creeks. Other violence followed in the tragic episode now known as the Chilcotin War, a historical drama filled with unforgettable characters. This is *The Chilcotin War*—a true tale of clashing cultures, greed, revenge and betrayal that is still controversial almost 150 years later.

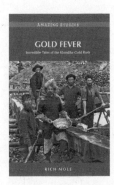

Gold Fever
Incredible Tales of the Klondike Gold Rush

print ISBN 978-1-894974-69-1
ebook ISBN 978-1-926936-21-5

In 1897, tens of thousands of would-be prospectors flooded into the Yukon in search of instant wealth during the Klondike Gold Rush. Enduring savage weather, unforgiving terrain, violence and starvation, a lucky few made their fortune, and some just as quickly lost it. The lure of the North is still irresistible in this exciting account of a fabled era of Canadian history.

Purchase Amazing Stories at your favourite bookstore or visit heritagehouse.ca to order online.

More Amazing Stories by Rich Mole

Rebel Women of the West Coast

Their Triumphs, Tragedies and Lasting Legacies

print ISBN 978-1-926613-28-4
ebook ISBN 978-1-926936-28-4

Here are the stories of West Coast women whose nonconformist beliefs and actions made them rebels in society's eyes. These vivid biographies profile celebrated women from British Columbia, Washington and Oregon, whose demands for equality in university lecture halls, shipyards, polling booths, government assemblies and operating theatres shaped the society we live in today.

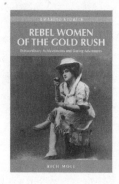

Rebel Women of the Gold Rush

Extraordinary Achievements and
Daring Adventures

print ISBN 978-1-894974-76-9
ebook ISBN 978-1-926613-88-8

During the Klondike Gold Rush, many daring women ventured north to seek riches and adventure. These unforgettable women defied the social conventions of the time and endured heartbreak and horrific conditions to build a life in the wild North. The Klondike's rebel women bring an intriguing new perspective to gold-rush history.

Purchase Amazing Stories at your favourite bookstore or visit heritagehouse.ca to order online.